ENGLISH 3
MATTERS

music facts!

ark
REAT
Y OUT!

SHOOTING STARS

MY BEST MOMENT
"Playing in Europe."

MY WORST MOMENT
"Getting injured last season and missing some games."

fashion update

CLARE CONSTANT · SUSAN DUBERLEY

Heinemann

Contents

*Spelling resource sheets will be found on pages 50–79
of the Teacher's File.*

Throughout this book you will find the following cross-references:

TRF The Teacher's File provides support for the activity.
PAGES 00–00

SKILLS The Skills Book offers skills practice related to the activity.
PAGES 00–00

SEE ALSO Other pages in the book will help you with the activity.
PAGES 00–00

The activities in this book have been colour coded:

- specific speaking and listening: pink

- reading: yellow

- writing: blue

- specific language work: dark blue

The money maze

1.1 | Work in pairs. This is your chance to take part in making a new family game show called *Stash your Cash*.

1.2 | Contestants have to answer questions. Write three question and answer cards on the subjects below for each of the three rounds.

| Round 1   Music | Round 2   TV | Round 3   Sport |

Each question must → begin with a capital letter and end with a question mark.

STASH YOUR CASH

Round 1 Subject: Music

Question: Whose number one hit was called 'Wonderwall'?

Answer: Oasis.

Each word in a proper name (names of people, places, teams) must begin with a ← capital letter.

1.3 | Work in pairs. Get ready to introduce your partner on the show. Work out what you will say. Make notes on answers to the following questions.

1 What is your name? Where are you from?

2 What are your interests/hobbies?

3 What is the most exciting thing you have ever done?

4 What is the funniest thing that has happened to you?

5 How would you spend the £1000 prize money?

1.4

SKILLS

PAGES 4–5

Work in groups of five. Act out your episode of *Stash your Cash*. One of you is the host. The others are two pairs of contestants. Follow the steps below. You may like to film or tape record your show.

This is Andy from Devon.
Andy really enjoys ...
Once he ...
The funniest thing ...
If he wins, Andy will spend ...

Step 1

Host welcomes the audience to tonight's *Stash your Cash* show:

> Welcome to tonight's exciting episode of ...

Step 2

Host asks each contestant to introduce his/her partner:

> Sanjay, please introduce your partner ...

Contestants introduce each other using their notes.

Step 3

For each round of questions:
Host says:

> This is round ... and the questions are all on ...

The host then asks each pair of contestants a question for that round. Do not ask the contestants the questions they wrote themselves!

The host keeps score of who gets the most right answers.

Contestants:
- must work together to answer each question quickly
- must not argue with the host or each other!

Step 4

Host at the end of the show announces the winners and gives them their £1000 prizes:

> ... and the winners of tonight's show with ... points are ...

1.5   Read the passage opposite. Dad promised Andrew not to tell him off at dinner. But Andrew spent 50 cents to try to make Dad break his promise.

1.6   Explain in your own words how Andrew tries to make Dad break his promise.

1.7   Work in pairs. Copy and complete the chart. Show how things become more tense as the story goes on.

Lines	What Andrew does	Dad's response	What Andrew thinks and feels about Dad
1–6	Picks up the chicken with his fingers and ...	Glares. Stares. Clears his throat.	Admiration: 'Doesn't crack. What a man. Nothing can ...'
7–11			
12–23			
24–27			He can see his Dad has nearly cracked. He knows that if he pushes Dad just a bit further ...
27–41			He knows his Dad will calm down. Then he'll tell him ...

1.8   Write Dad's diary entry about what happened. Show how he became angrier and angrier. Use your chart to help you. Begin your diary like this.

TRF
PAGE 12
SKILLS
PAGES 6–7

> I made a big mistake today. I promised Andrew ... I thought nothing would make me break ... When we sat down to ... I couldn't believe my eyes. Andrew ...

Licked

I pick up the chicken with my fingers and start stuffing it into my mouth. I have never seen anyone look mad the way Dad looks at me. He glares. He stares. He clears his throat. But he
5 doesn't crack. What a man. Nothing can make him break his promise.

I snap a chicken bone in half and suck out the middle. It is hollow and I can see right through it. I suck and slurp and swallow. Dad is going red in
10 the face. Little veins are standing out on his nose. But still he does not crack.

The last course is baked apple and custard. I will get him with that. I put the hollow bone into the custard and use it like a straw. I suck the custard up
15 the chicken bone.

Dad clears his throat. He is very red in the face. 'Andrew,' he says.

He is going to crack. I have won.

'Yes,' I say through a mouthful of custard.

20 'Nothing,' he mumbles.

Dad is terrific. He is under enormous pressure but still he keeps his cool. There is only one thing left to do. I take out my secret weapon.

I place the yellow fly swat on the table next to
25 my knife. Dad looks at it lying there on the white tablecloth. He stares and stares and stares. But nothing is said. I pick up the fly swat and start to lick it. I lick it like an ice-cream. A bit of chewy brown goo comes off my tongue. I swallow it
30 quickly. Then I crunch on a bit of crispy black stuff.

Dad stands up. It is too much for him. He cracks. 'Aaaaaagh,' he screams. He charges at me with hands held out like claws.

I run for it. I run down to my room and lock the
35 door. Dad yells and shouts. He kicks and screams. But I lie low.

Tomorrow, when he calms down, I'll own up. I'll tell him how I went down the street and bought a new fly swat for fifty cents. I'll tell him about the
40 currants and little bits of liquorice that I smeared on the fly swat.

Adapted from *Licked* by Paul Jennings

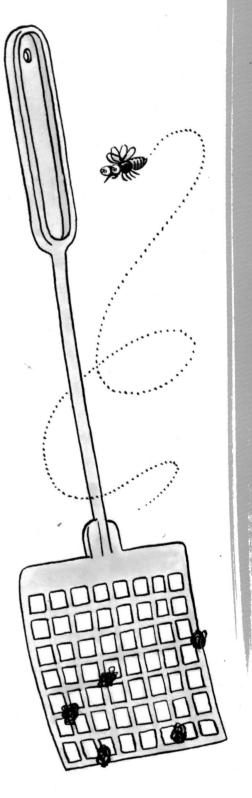

1.9 Read the article opposite from *Shout* magazine about looking after your money. Answer the questions below.

1.10 Work in pairs. What order do you think the tips should be in? Make the most useful 1 and the least useful 7.

> For example: 1 = G

1.11 The writer of this magazine article has written it in a chatty, informal way and uses slang. Read lines 1–6 and 23–26.

1 Write down **two** informal words which mean 'money'.

2 Write down **two** other phrases which are informal.

1.12 Choose one of the money-earning ideas in lines 26–29. Then answer the questions below to help you plan a flyer to advertise your service.

1 What will you do?

2 Why would you be a good person to use? Write a paragraph using some of the words below. Choose some of your own.

| reliable | punctual | experienced | patient |
| hard-working | tidy | energetic | sensible |

3 How much do you charge?

4 How can someone get in touch with you?

1.13 Now write your flyer. It should sound serious. After all, you want people to give you work!

Heaps of ways to get more for your money!

GET RICH TIPS

Everything would seem so much better if you had **limitless** piles of cash to spare, wouldn't it? It would be great if you could buy as many clothes and CDs as you wanted. Think of all the sports gear you could buy and all the places you could go to – cool! But we live in the real world, where the only answer is to learn to budget your cash ...

A Try not to **fritter** money away. You might not think that spending 50p on sweets a day is a lot, but if you saved that 50p and took a snack from home instead, imagine how much money you could save ...

B If your pocket money just isn't stretching, offer to do some extra chores in return for a rise!

C Always try to have a little fund for 'emergencies', so you don't get stuck somewhere.

D Send off for free samples.

E Become a bargain hunter – you can really become an expert! Don't pay the full price for clothes if you can help it.

F Although you have to be 15 or over to land yourself a Saturday job, there are heaps of other ways to earn some dosh. What about dog-walking, lawn-mowing, car-washing, or if you're confident with children, helping at children's parties?

G If you're hopeless at saving and have to spend every penny you have every week, don't keep your cash in the house. Instead open a new bank or building society account for savings. Don't take a cash card if they offer you one. Knowing you can get cash from a machine on a Saturday afternoon is just gonna be too much temptation.

Save £££s!

Adapted from *Shout* magazine

limitless – endless   **fritter** – waste little by little

1.14

Read the poem opposite. It was written by a homeless person. Then answer the questions below.

1.15

Work in a group.

1 Read the first stanza (verse). Who might the poet be talking to? Give reasons.

2 Read lines 1–5. What is the poet asking people to think about?

3 Now read lines 6–9. Do you think most people are really too poor to give to a beggar? Why might people not be able to give?

4 Read lines 10–15. Name **two** differences between the ways that a homeless person and a consumer might live.

5 Read lines 16–19. What would the homeless person like? Why?

1.16

Does the poem make you want to give money to homeless people or not? Why?

1.17

SKILLS
PAGES 8–9

Write about the poem. Use the work you have done to help you.

1 Explain what each stanza is about.

2 Which words or phrases make you imagine what it is like to be homeless? Explain why.

3 Say whether you think the poem would make people want to give money to homeless people. Give reasons.

How much?

Have you got enough
Will you get by?
Can you survive the week ahead?
What about the little luxuries
5   And all those special treats?
Can you spare a bit for charity
For the beggar at the end of the street?
Or will you tighten your belt and try to
Make ends meet?

10   Will you go and be a **consumer** this week?
Or will you tramp the street, letting
water into your feet?
Money makes the world go round
Whether you live in a luxury flat
15   Or sleep on the street
Oh for the feeling of a wallet full of
Notes with **freedom of security**
Rather than a pocketful of copper
And a **life of uncertainty**

By Pete, Brighton

consumer – someone who can afford to buy things

freedom of security – feeling safe because you have enough money to pay for things

life of uncertainty – never being sure what is going to happen to you

Pronouns

1.18

Read the passage below.

> **We** were having a PC Game competition at our Youth Club. The game was 'Dargar 3'. **It** is a really tricky game. If **you** had the highest score **you** won £30. **I** really wanted to win but **I** was playing against Peter. **He** wins most of the time. But **he** has got 'Dargar 3' on a computer at home and **I** haven't.

The words in bold are called **pronouns**. The following words are all pronouns: I   you   he   she   it   we   they.

The pronouns *he, she, it, we* and *they* can be used instead of a noun or noun phrase:

Peter wins most of the time. ⟶ **He** wins most of the time.

1.19

TRF

PAGE 13

Now write out and complete the sentences below. Use each pronoun from the box once.

1 At the start of 'Dargar 3' _____ both crash land on the planet Dargar.

2 You are trying to collect fuel. You need _____ to get home.

3 You can run out of oxygen and you will die without _____ .

4 You need to find the King so _____ can give you more oxygen.

5 There are lots of monsters and _____ can steal from you or kill you.

   you   he   it   they   it

Keep it clear

1.20

Look at the cartoon and read the sentences about it. Then read the box below.

1 He was really fed up because he was losing. 2 Mike was really fed up because Mike was losing.

1 Can you tell who is fed up in sentence 1?

It is confusing when people use too many pronouns in their writing. The reader cannot work out what is going on. Always use enough names to make it clear who or what you are talking about:

Mike was really fed up because he was losing.

2 Where could the writer of sentence 2 use a pronoun to make it easier to read?

If it is clear who or what you are talking about, use a pronoun instead of repeating a noun. This will make your work easier to read:

*Mike was really fed up because **he** was losing.*

1.21

TRF
PAGE 14
SKILLS
PAGE 10

Rewrite the paragraph below. Change the words in bold so it clearly says what is happening. Use nouns and pronouns correctly. Choose words from the box.

Mike loses the game. Carla gives Peter the prize of £30. Peter and Mike have been saving up for a trip to Alton Towers. Peter will put the money towards it.

Peter and Mike were playing a computer game. **Peter and Mike** were in a competition. As his spaceman was killed, **he** knew he had lost. **He** was excited about winning. **She** gave **it** to Peter and said **Peter** had done well. Peter knew what he would spend **it** on. **They** would go to Alton Towers on Saturday.

Mike
they
he
Carla
the prize
Peter
He and Mike
the money

UNIT 2 | How healthy?

2.1 Read the passage opposite. Cameron has a serious heart problem. His only chance is if Dr Bryce tries a risky new transplant operation. Cameron has to decide what to do.

2.2 Read lines 8–18. Write a paragraph explaining what you learn about the transplant Cameron might have.

2.3 Work in pairs. How do Cameron's thoughts and feelings change as he thinks about whether to have the operation? Use a chart like the one below.

Lines	Cameron's thoughts	His feelings
3	He must make a decision now.	He's been dreading this moment.
19–22	He wishes he could ... but there isn't time ...	He is worried about ...
23–28	He will ... because ...	He's aware he doesn't really have a choice if ... He's aware that his parents are ...

2.4

SKILLS

PAGES 12–13

Work in pairs. One of you is Cameron. The other is a television reporter interviewing him about the operation.

1 Work out five questions the reporter will ask. Think about:

- what the operation involves
- how his mum and dad each feels
- how Cameron feels
- why he wants the operation.

2 Work out Cameron's answers.

3 Rehearse and present the interview in small groups or on tape.

Time to decide

'It's entirely up to you, Cameron. Your parents may sign the
consent forms but it's your decision.' Dr Bryce smiled.

This was it. The moment I'd been waiting for and dreading.

'While Cameron's thinking about it, what about you two,
5 Mr and Mrs Kelsey? How do you feel about it?'

'I have every confidence in you, Doctor,' Dad gushed.

'I want whatever Cameron wants,' Mum replied quietly.

'How many **genetically engineered** pigs have you got altogether?' I
asked.

10 'We have over a hundred, but only about twenty are suitable for
human organ donation.'

'D'you know which pig you'd use for the **transplant**?'

Dr Bryce nodded. 'We have two pigs who are particularly suitable –
their names are Paul and Trudy – but I think we'd use Trudy. She's
15 very special. I think she's our best bet. And once the first transplant is
a success, there'd be nothing stopping us doing more. But Cameron,
you have to decide whether or not you want to be the first one to
undergo this operation.'

First ... I'd rather be second or third or fourth. That way any
20 mistakes they made in the first operation could be put right for the
next ones. But I didn't have time left to slip any further down the
queue. It was go first or not at all.

'I think ... I think, yes. I would like to be considered for the
transplant,' I decided.

25 'I'll make some tea.' Mum left the room abruptly.

I looked at my dad, who looked down at the carpet.

'Dr Bryce, I'd like the transplant very much,' I said. 'It's quite
simple really. I want to live.'

Adapted from *Pig-Heart Boy* by Malorie Blackman

---

consent forms – legal papers agreeing to the operation

genetically engineered – the pigs have been altered so their
hearts will work in humans

human organ donation – the heart grown in the pig will be given
to a human

transplant – the operation to replace the sick person's heart with
the heart grown in the pig

2.5 Read the poem opposite. The person in the poem cannot hear because his ears are full of wax. A nurse is going to wash them out.

2.6 Copy and complete the chart below showing ten noises described in the poem. Say how the descriptions help you to understand the poem.

Noises	Description	Effect
other people's voices (line 1)	wrapped in cotton wool	it makes you 'hear' the voices as muffled and dull
my voice (line 2)	...	...

2.7

SKILLS
PAGE 14

Some words in the poem *sound* like the noise they describe (such as *hissed*). This is called *onomatopoeia* (say onna-matta-pee-a).

1 Circle at least three words in your chart that sound like the thing they describe.

2 The words you have circled use onomatopoeia. How do they help you get a clearer picture of what is being described?

3 Write down three words, not in the poem, which use onomatopoeia.

2.8

SKILLS
PAGE 15

The poem also has words near each other beginning with the same letter sounds: *p*umped and *p*ulsing in lines 4–5. This is called *alliteration*.

1 Copy out lines 13 and 16–18. Underline the alliteration.

2 How does the use of alliteration help you get a clearer picture of what is being described?

2.9 Describe a visit to a dentist. Use onomatopoeia and alliteration to make it lively. Use the box below and a dictionary to help you.

My trembling teeth chattered as I entered the dentist's door ...

dentist's drill drummed   ouch   rattled   grinding gums

Having My Ears Done

People's voices were wrapped in cotton wool.
My own rattled in a closed tunnel.
'See Nurse,' said the Doctor.

She pumped water in my ears
5 Pulsing like an outboard motor.
It ran out with a crackle.

The world came alive and **imploded**.
'OK?' said Nurse. 'Don't shout,' I said.
'My normal voice,' she answered.

10 In the waiting room,
Opened newspapers cracked like thunder.
Footsteps on the floor were bells ringing.

My anorak spat out electric sparks.
And jeans hissed together.
15 Shoes creaked like old doors.

Outside, birds chirping their heads off
Were steel chisels striking stone.
I could even hear the grass grow.

By Robert Sparrow

imploded – burst inwards (the opposite of exploded)

2.10

Read the advertisement opposite. Then work in a group and answer the questions below.

1 Read lines 1–15. Who is meant to read the advertisement? How do you know?

2 Read lines 16–35. What does the advertisement say about acids? What does it want the reader to believe about Ribena Tooth Kind?

3 What does the picture make you think about Ribena Tooth Kind?

4 Look at the heading and lines 36–39 of the advertisement. What is the advertisement bringing to people's attention? Why?

2.11

The advertisement uses facts (things that can be proved true) to help make people want to buy Ribena Tooth Kind. List five facts from the advertisement.

> 1 A child in the UK gets through …

2.12

What might the advertisement make parents worry about? List three things. Look at lines 1–10, 16–21 and 22–24.

2.13

TRF

PAGE 16

Explain how the advertisement tries to persuade readers to buy Ribena Tooth Kind. Use the plan below to help you.

1 The advertisement is meant to be read by …

2 The advertisement claims that …

3 It impresses readers by telling them these facts …

4 It may worry readers by ….

5 The picture makes the reader think that …

6 I think people *will/will not* buy Ribena Tooth Kind after reading this advertisement because …

There is only one soft drink accredited by the British Dental Association

If you're a mum or dad, what you're about to read will put your teeth on edge.

A child in the UK gets through,
5 on average, about a litre of soft drinks a day.

A Children's Dental Health Survey was carried out in 1993. It showed that 54% of twelve-year-
10 olds have filled, decayed or missing teeth.

Buying your children a No Added Sugar soft drink is a step in the right direction, but sugar is only
15 part of the problem.

NEW THREAT TO TEETH

Dentists now believe that the *acids* in our diet can cause **dental erosion**.

Basically, these acids can slowly
20 dissolve enamel from the surface of teeth.

THE SCALE OF THE PROBLEM

Nearly a third of 14-year-olds suffer from erosion of their second teeth.

25

KEEP SMILING

Naturally we have a suggestion that should keep a smile on everyone's face: New Ribena Tooth Kind.

Tooth Kind offers all the fresh blackcurranty taste and Vitamin C 30 goodness of Ribena, but has no added sugar and is **substantially** lower in fruit acids too.

Scientists have proved that it does not encourage tooth erosion. 35 This impressed the British Dental Association: Ribena Tooth Kind is the first and only soft drink to receive BDA accreditation.

Ribena Tooth Kind is a registered trademark

---

accredited – approved of   **dental erosion** – wearing away of teeth
substantially – much

Audience and purpose

2.14

Read these three texts. Then answer the questions below.

A

THERE WILL BE A FAIR IN KING'S PARK ON SATURDAY 23RD JULY AT 2.00PM.

Your youngsters can enjoy a treasure hunt, Teddy Bears' picnic, a bouncy castle, a fun fair and lots of stalls.

B

Are you fit, over 18 and looking for the adventure of a lifetime?

If so, volunteer to be one of Heartbeat's sponsored cyclists. You may be chosen to cycle the length of the Nile in August and raise money for heart transplants. Volunteer now and find out more.

C

Once upon a time there were three bears: a Mummy Bear, a Daddy Bear and the littlest, tiniest Baby Bear you've ever seen ...

2.15

Which passage is meant to be read by:

1 a child   2 fit adults   3 parents?

2.16

Decide what each passage above is trying to do for the reader.

1 Which passage is entertaining the reader?

2 Which passage is persuading the reader to do something?

3 Which passage is giving the reader information?

Every piece of writing is meant to be read by someone. The readers it is aimed at are called its **audience**. A piece of writing for a young child will be different from a piece of writing for an adult.

Every piece of writing is trying to do something. The thing it is trying to do is called its **purpose**. Something written to entertain will be different from something written to inform.

2.17

TRF
PAGE 17

Work in pairs. Read the passages below, then answer the questions.

A

Football training for Year 12 pupils is at 4.00pm on the field. Full kit must be worn, especially football boots. Anyone wearing trainers will be sent home.

B

Join Heart to Heart Dating Agency and meet the partner of your dreams. We take great care to make sure couples are well suited. Go on, you've nothing to lose! Your dream date is waiting. Find out more by phoning 01745 454353. (You must be over 18.)

C

COMEDIAN: Have you heard about the man who goes into a pub carrying a large bit of tarmac?

'What would you like, sir?' says the bar tender.

The man says, 'Two pints please. One for me and *one for the road*!'

1 Who is the audience for each piece of writing? How do you know?

2 What is the purpose of each piece of writing? How do you know?

If you know the audience and purpose of a piece of writing then you can work out

* **why** the author wrote it like that
* **how** well the piece of writing succeeds.

2.18

SKILLS
PAGES 16–19

Would this advertisement make younger teenagers want to join the health club? Give reasons for your answer.

Fit not Fat — Join today!

We offer:
✦ keep fit classes to help get your shape back
✦ good value daytime membership
✦ a crèche for babies and young children
✦ a friendly atmosphere where you can make new friends.

Persuasive language

Read the advertisement below.

FEELING RUN DOWN?
NEED SOME EXTRA ENERGY?

You need

Vitatonic!

Vitatonic contains all the vitamins and minerals your body needs, plus five special herbs to give you that extra boost. — 5

It has a delicious taste and you'll notice a difference within hours! You'll be full of dazzling energy and sparkling happiness. — 10 ... 15

Try Vitatonic!
Only £1.99, but what a difference it makes!

2.20 Write down *five* words or phrases which make taking Vitatonic seem a good idea.

2.21

TRF
PAGE 18

When writers want to persuade readers, they may use adjectives, facts and opinions. Look again at the words or phrases you chose.

1 Write down any adjectives (words which describe nouns).

  1 special (line 8)

2 Circle any facts (information you can check is true).

  1 Vitatonic contains all the vitamins and ...

3 Underline any opinions (someone's point of view).

  1 You need Vitatonic!

2.22 Write a paragraph explaining how the advertisement persuades readers to try Vitatonic. Use your work on adjectives, facts and opinions to help you.

2.23 | Read the following article.

Tasty and tempting though they are, burgers, chips, crisps, sweets and fizzy drinks don't contain all the goodness your body needs. If you want to look good and feel fantastic then give your body all the help you can.

5 **Eat fresh fruit and vegetables every day. They're delicious!**

A baked potato with cheese and a salad is an ideal lunch.

An apple, banana or orange is a great
10 snack if you are feeling peckish or need an energy boost.

Get that protein inside you. You'll feel great!

Meat, fish, cheese, eggs ... it's up to you.
15 Protein is the building block that helps your body grow into great shape.

Drink lots of cool, clear water. It's so refreshing!

Eight glasses a day will make your skin clear
20 and your eyes sparkle. (And you never know who'll notice!)

Cut out some of the nasties – you don't need them.

Greasy chips, fatty crisps, sugary cakes and
25 biscuits – yeah, they're fine ... once in a while. But have them every day and they fill you up, pile on weight, and rot your teeth! And they don't give your body the
30 vitamins and minerals it needs to keep you looking fab.

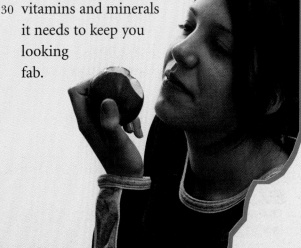

2.24 | Work in a group. How does the article persuade teenagers to eat healthy food?

1 Find three adjectives which are used to persuade.

2 Find three facts which are used to persuade.

3 Find three opinions which are used to persuade.

2.25 | Write about the article. Explain how it tries to persuade the reader. Use the work you have done to help you.

Party! Party!

UNIT 3

3.1 Ellie is being picked on by some skinheads at a party. Read the passage opposite. Then, in your own words, explain how Dan rescues Ellie.

3.2 Now look at what happened more carefully.

1 Read lines 27–38. What did Dan think would make the skinheads leave?

2 When do you think Dan had the idea to put wine punch on his shirt?

3 Read lines 3–9. How does Dan feel about Ellie? How do you know?

3.3 Work in groups of four (Ellie, Dan, the skinhead and Sandy). Act out the story. Only mime lines 11–12!

3.4 Write the story from Dan's point of view. Include:

TRF
PAGE 20

1 what the skinheads were like

2 how Dan feels about Ellie

3 how Dan works out how to rescue Ellie

4 what happened when Dan carried out his plan.

> I was at a party with Ellie. A skinhead came over and asked her to dance. She didn't want to but the skinhead wouldn't go away. He grabbed Ellie. I had to do something. But what? I said something stupid like, 'Are you deaf or ...

My hero!

The skinhead's hanging on to me. 'You come and have a little dance with me and my mates.'

'She's with me. Are you deaf or something?' Dan says desperately.

'Dan! It's OK. Don't argue with him,' I hiss, because I'm so scared there might be a fight. They could have knives.

'There! She *wants* to dance, don't you, sweetheart?' he says, and puts his arms round me, his horrible beery breath hot on my cheek. 'That's it – let's get cosy, eh?'

'Leave her alone!' Dan shouts, jumping up.

'Shut him up, eh, Sandy,' the skinhead says.

The heaviest of his mates lumbers over to Dan. There's a thud, a squeal, and then Dan is sprawling on the floor.

'Dan!'

'Shut up or you'll get it too,' says the skin. 'Did you pop him one, Sandy?'

'Help!' Dan screams, staggering up. His white T-shirt is stained dark red. 'He's stabbed me! I'm bleeding, look!'

Screams echo right round the room as Dan lurches forwards and then sinks to his knees.

'What have you done now, Sandy? Quick! Run for it!' the skinhead yells, shoving me aside and taking to his heels. The others follow him. No one dares stop them.

'Dan!' I say, bending down, clutching him, trying to prop his head on my knees. 'Someone dial 999, and get an ambulance!'

'It's OK,' says Dan, trying to sit up. 'I don't need an ambulance.'

'Are you *crazy*? You've been stabbed!'

'No I haven't,' says Dan, grinning. 'Those thugs have gone, haven't they? I thought they might run for it if they thought I was bleeding to death. I don't think that guy even had a knife. He just punched me in the stomach and I fell over.'

'But the blood!'

'Smell it,' says Dan, holding out his sopping T-shirt.

'Yuck!'

'It's the wine punch. I spilled it all over me.'

Adapted from *girls in love* by Jacqueline Wilson

3.5 Read the newspaper article opposite. When Emma's parents went away it seemed like a great chance to hold a party.

3.6 Which of the points below led to the vandalism happening? Explain why.

> 1 Mr and Mrs Cooke left Emma alone for 24 hours.
>
> 2 Emma behaved as her parents expected her to.
>
> 3 A lot of alcohol was drunk by the teenagers.
>
> 4 The family could not claim £6000 on the insurance.
>
> 5 The teenagers who came to the party behaved badly.

3.7 Work in pairs. No one wants their party to end like Emma's. How can you stop it? Complete a spider diagram like the one below.

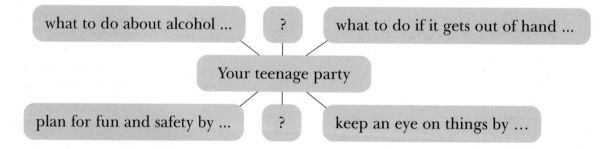

3.8 Work on your own. Write a leaflet to persuade parents that it is possible to have a safe teenage party at home. Use the plan below.

Panel 1	Panel 2	Panel 3	Panel 4
Your teenage party – it needn't be hell!		Write about planning and holding the party.	Say what to do if it all goes wrong.

Teenager's parents leave her alone for the first time ... and return to find house trashed

By CHRIS BROOKE

When Terence and Jennifer Cooke left their 16-year-old daughter alone at home for the first time, they felt sure everything would be fine.

They were only going to be away for 24 hours, they reasoned, and she was a 'quiet and shy' girl who was sure to act responsibly. But they were wrong – and it proved an expensive mistake.

Hours after they left, Emma threw a party for friends which spiralled out of control. Teenagers consumed the contents of the drinks cabinet, then worked around the family's three-bedroom semi, vandalising every room. This was the damage:

Kitchen: Tomato sauce, chutney, mayonnaise and spaghetti thrown across units, ceiling and floor.

Lounge: Cigarette burns on coffee table, sofa, chair and carpet. Hi-fi wrecked.

Hall: Cooking oil splashed across hall and stairway carpet and food everywhere. A dried flower arrangement with sentimental value torn to shreds. Shaving foam and washing up liquid on stairway walls.

Main bedroom: Covered in broken eggs thrown everywhere. One teenager had been sick on the floor.

Son's bedrooom: Carpet stained and wallpaper torn.

Daughter's bedroom: Cereals and food thrown all over.

Bathroom: Total mess, with shaving foam and shower gel on the walls and carpet.

To add insult to injury, the Cookes could not reclaim the £6000 damage on their insurance because the vandals had not broken into the house.

Adapted from *The Daily Mail*, 24 June 1998

3.9 Work in a group. You are going to give a reading of the poem opposite. First read the poem aloud. Note down your answers to these questions.

1 Which stanzas are quick to read? Which words or phrases are repeated in those stanzas?

2 Which stanzas are slower? Which words make those stanzas slower?

3 What do the following words from the poem tell you about?

rip   jerk   move   dip   spin   shift   stride   glide

4 Which words best describe this poem? Why?

lazy   lively   cheerful   sad   funny

3.10 In your group, practise your reading of the poem. Make sure listeners can hear the beat (rhythm) of the poem. You could add actions and sound effects. Then present your poem to the other groups or tape-record it.

3.11 Write your own poem about eating. Use a thesaurus to find as many eating verbs as you can. Follow the pattern below.

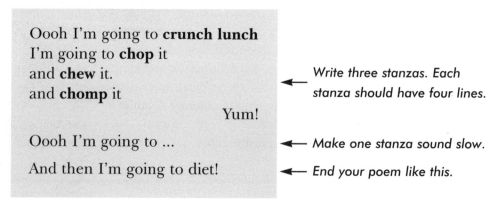

Oooh I'm going to **crunch lunch**
I'm going to **chop** it
and **chew** it.
and **chomp** it
                        Yum!

Oooh I'm going to ...

And then I'm going to diet!

← Write three stanzas. Each stanza should have four lines.

← Make one stanza sound slow.

← End your poem like this.

Break Dance

I'm going to break/dance
turn rippling glass
stretch my muscles to the bass

5   I'm going to break/dance
I'm going to rip it
and jerk it
and take it apart

I'm going to chop it
10 and move it
and groove it

Oooh I'm going to ooze it
electric boogaloo
electric boogaloo
15 across your floor

I'm going to break/dance
watch my ass
take the shine
off your laugh
20

I'm going to dip it
and spin it
let my spine twist it
I'm going to shift it
25 and stride it
let my mind glide it

Then I'm going to ease it
ease it
and bring it all home

30 believing in the beat
believing in the beat
of myself

By Grace Nichols

Whoo!

Whoo!

SEE ALSO

PAGE 92

Using quotations

Copying words from a text into your work is called **quoting**.

You can use quotations when you are answering a question about a text. The quote will show which part of the text made you give your answer.

Page 92 shows you how quotations should be set out.

3.12

First read the following passage. Darren wants to hold a party.

'It'll only be some of the people from my year, like Nissa, and Gary, and Dave. Nothing will go wrong.' Darren was careful to name his three quietest friends.

'Yeah? Look what happened to Emma's house. It was wrecked. Her party cost that family thousands. Forget it, Darren!' His dad's face was turning grey just at the thought of all the money the Cookes had to spend fixing their home after Emma's party had got out of hand.

'Oh Dad!' Darren moaned. Why wouldn't Dad even listen? There was no way his friends would wreck his house.

3.13

SKILLS

PAGES 20–21

Now write out the word or phrase which shows you that:

1 Darren is being careful about what he says.

2 Dad feels scared about what could go wrong.

3 Darren feels his dad is being unfair.

Using quotations and explaining details

3.14 Read the following passage. Dad has just walked into Darren's party.

> '*What* is going on?' Dad's shocked yell could barely be heard above the throbbing music and shrill screams. Surely that wasn't Nissa Patel squirting a shaving foam heart onto a boy's head?
>
> 'Er ... hi, Mr Jones.' Nissa dropped the can as if it was in flames. Darren had said his dad was away. From the look on Mr Jones' face they had better make a quick exit.

3.15 Write a sentence for each statement below. Use a quotation that shows that:

1 The noise from the party is loud.

The words 'Dad's ...' show that ...

2 Dad is surprised by Nissa's behaviour.

3 Nissa feels guilty about what she is doing.

When you have found a part of the text which shows *why* you have given your answer to a question, then:

- carefully choose which words to quote
- explain how they prove your point.

You can tell Nissa feels guilty because the passage says she:
   '... dropped the can as if it was in flames ...'
The words:
   'as if it was in flames'
show how strong her feelings were. She doesn't just put the can down. She drops it quickly as if it is burning her hand.

3.16

TRF
PAGE 21

Now look at the phrases you quoted above. Explain how they prove your point.

Possessive pronouns

3.17

Read the sentences below. Write down the word from the box you should use to fill the gap in each sentence.

> 1 'Stay at _____ house, the rave is just down the road from me,' Rick told Simon.
>
> 2 'Is _____ sister going?' Simon asked hopefully.
>
> 3 'Yes, and _____ boyfriend is going too,' Rick warned.
>
> | your | her | my |
> | --- | --- | --- |

The words you used are all **possessive pronouns**.

Remember that a pronoun stands in for a noun:

The rave *is great fun.*   ***It*** *is great fun.*

A possessive pronoun stands in for people or things that have or own something:

*stay with me at **my** house.*

my shows it is Rick's house.

These are all possessive pronouns:

	1			2		
Singular:	my	your	his her its	mine	yours	his hers
Plural:	our	your	their	ours	yours	theirs

The possessive pronouns in column 1 are sometimes known as possessive adjectives.

TRF
PAGE 19

3.18

Now list the possessive pronouns in the sentences below.

> 1 As they danced, their faces became red and sweaty.
>
> 2 'My water's finished. May I have some of yours?' Rick asked.
>
> 3 Sheri gave him some of hers.

3.19

Copy the sentences below. Choose the correct possessive pronoun from the box to fill the blank in each sentence.

1 After the rave people were searching for _____ coats.

2 'I can't see any of _____ jackets,' Rick moaned.

3 'Hurry up, you two,' Simon said as he found _____.

4 'Look, Rick, _____ is over there under _____,' Sheri said.

5 Rick passed Sheri _____ and they left.

| mine | yours | his | hers | our | their |

3.20

TRF
PAGE 22
SKILLS
PAGE 22

A photograph of Rick and his friends at the rave appeared in the local newspaper. Finish writing what they said about it. Make sure each speech has a possessive pronoun in it.

1 'Look! _____ photograph is in the paper!' Rick said.

2 'That sister of _____ looks great,' Simon said.

3 'Is that copy of the newspaper _____ ?' Sheri asked.

4 'We'd better hide it before _____ parents see it!' said Rick.

UNIT 4 Wild about animals

4.1 Read the passage opposite. Billy is a teenager. He is hunting the Beast – a panther that has been killing local farmers' sheep.

4.2 Say whether each of the following sentences about the passage is true or false. Give reasons.

1 Billy has come prepared to shoot the panther.

2 Billy only sees the panther following him.

3 Aggerton Moss is warm, dry and safe.

4 The panther is chasing after Billy.

4.3 Work in pairs. List six clues that show Billy feels more and more scared as the story goes on.

1 In lines 3–4 he thinks, 'I daren't make a sound.'
2 In lines 9–10 ...

4.4 Work in pairs. Think of three different ways the story could end.

4.5 Work on your own. Choose the best ending. Write it in three paragraphs. Show Billy's thoughts and feelings.

SKILLS
PAGES 24–25

I was terrified but ... I thought ...

The Nature of the Beast

I couldn't see anything now, except the humps of grass and all the **tussocks** either side of the road looking like things crouching. I started to unwrap my air rifle, but I daren't make a sound.

5   There were no trees, nowhere to run to. And no sound of a car. I didn't know how fast panthers can run, but I knew it would be faster than me.

There were no trees, nowhere to run to. And no sound of a car. I didn't know how fast panthers can run, but I knew it would be faster than me.

Then I heard the sound, softer than a real sound almost. Padding. It was hard to hear because my heart
10   was beating that loud. Coming towards me, down the dark slope of the road.

There's no way I can describe how scared I was.

And suddenly I dropped my bag and made a run for it, tearing the dustbin liner off my air rifle. Maybe I
15   yelled. I can't remember. I can only remember running – not back the way I'd come, but sideways, into the marsh and peat of Aggerton Moss.

And, behind me, I could hear it, softly, almost daintily, padding along on big cat feet. Even without looking, I
20   could see the way it would spring from tussock to tussock, jumping peaty streams. I was wading through those streams, half sinking up to my knees, with the icy water making me want to scream.

And the Beast wasn't even trying. It was just loping
25   along.

I didn't just think I might die – I knew I was going to. I'd never see Dad again.

Adapted from *The Nature of the Beast* by Janni Howker

tussocks – clumps of grass

35

4.6

TRF
PAGE 24

Is it cruel to use animals in films and on television? Read the views opposite. Then answer the questions below.

4.7

Work in pairs. Which views are *for* and which views are *against* animals being used as actors?

4.8

Work in pairs. Which view would you use to *disagree* with each statement below? Why?

1 If a baby chimpanzee starts acting in advertisements there's a long, golden future ahead of it.

2 You can tell the animals are well-treated by how they act.

3 Protected species are never used as actor animals.

4 Filming is boring and stressful for animals, so they're better off living in a zoo.

5 Animals don't need to be shown in a film about real life.

4.9

Work on your own. Write at least four paragraphs about whether animals should be used as actors. Use your own words – don't copy out the views opposite! Explain:

1 What sorts of things animal actors are used for. Give examples of programmes you have seen.

2 Why some people think it is all right for animals to act.

3 Why some people do not think animals should act.

4 What your views are about using animal actors.

Free to act?

A People keep pets because they enjoy them. People spend time watching animals and birds as a hobby. People go to zoos, safari parks and circuses to be amused by animals. So what's the problem with using animals in films or on television to entertain people?

B Advertisers like PG Tips only use chimpanzees when they are babies and cute. Once they grow up they are too tame to go into the wild. They don't have a future.

C Animals enjoy the love and attention they get from their trainers, and the fun of trying out new things and doing a job well. Acting is a much more rewarding life than sitting in a zoo cage and being stared at for hours on end.

D Knowing film makers will pay well for animal actors makes smugglers greedy – even if the animals are a protected species and might become extinct. In 1993 an orang-utan was illegally caught in the wild and imported from Indonesia. It was used in a PG Tips advertisement.

F You never see how an animal has been trained – only how it acts on screen. All kinds of cruel things may have been done to get it to perform like that.

E Animals are part of everyday life so they should be shown in television programmes and films about real life. Most of the animals used as actors are bred from captive animals so they're not wild, and they never would be.

4.10

Read the poem opposite. Then answer the questions below.

1 Where are the foxes playing? (*lines 1–8*)

2 Why is the vixen being so watchful? (*lines 5–10*)

3 Why might a horseman who *stops still* be dangerous? (*line 7*)

4 Why might the other humans be a danger to the foxes? (*lines 9–10*)

4.11

Work in a group. Look at the detail in the poem.

1 Read lines 3–4 and 7–8. How can you tell the vixen is more scared in lines 7–8?

2 Read lines 3–4, 7–8 and 13–14. How is the cubs' behaviour different from their mother's? Why do you think this is?

4.12

This type of poem is called a *sonnet*. A sonnet is a poem with fourteen lines and a regular pattern. Find the pattern.

1 Look at the end of each line. Which lines rhyme?

2 How many syllables (beats) are there in each line?

4.13

Now use the above information to write three short paragraphs about John Clare's poem.

Paragraph 1: Describe what picture he gave you of the family of foxes.

In John Clare's poem 'The Vixen' he describes a vixen ...

Paragraph 2: Give some details he used to make the poem interesting.

Paragraph 3: Describe the pattern he made his poem follow.

The Vixen

vixen – female fox

Among the taller wood with ivy hung,

The old fox plays and dances round her young.

She snuffs and barks if any passes by

And swings her tail and turns prepared to fly.

5 The horseman hurries by, she bolts to see,

And turns **agen**, from danger never free.   again

If **any stands** she runs among the **poles**   horseman stops still   tree trunks

And barks and snaps and drives **them** in the holes.   the young foxes

The shepherd sees **them** and the boy goes by   the foxes

10 And gets a stick and **progs** the hole to try.   prods

They get all still and lie in safety sure,

And out again when everything's secure,

And start and snap at blackbirds bouncing by

To fight and catch the great white butterfly.

By John Clare

Different types of sentences

4.14

First read through these sentences.

1 Agent Mulder **measured** a strange footprint.

2 Scully **was watching** from the woods behind him.

3 She **heard** something odd and **called** Mulder.

4 Perhaps something **was following** them, or perhaps she **was imagining** it.

5 Mulder **photographed** the footprint and he **rushed** over to Scully.

4.15

TRF
PAGE 25

Now sort the above sentences into two groups:

A **Those with one verb or verb phrase** Sentence 1	B **Those with more than one verb or verb phrase** Sentence 3

A group of words with one complete verb or verb phrase is called a **clause**.

*Agent Mulder **measured** a strange footprint.*
                    |
                  verb

Sentences with only one clause are called **simple sentences**.

Sentences which have more than one clause are called **multiple sentences**.

*She **heard** something odd* and ***called** Mulder.*
clause 1   clause 2

Multiple sentences can be compound or complex sentences.

Compound sentences

4.16

First read the sentences below.

> **1** Mulder chased the monster and he saw its face.
>
> **2** It was getting very dark but he knew it was an alien.
>
> **3** Scully might believe him or she might still have doubts.

4.17

Now break each sentence above into clauses. Which word is left over?

> For example, sentence 1:
> *Clause 1*   Mulder chased the monster
> *Clause 2*   he saw its face.
> *Word left over:*   and

> The sentences you broke up were **compound sentences**.
> Compound sentences are made up of clauses often joined
> together with these **connectives** (joining words):
> and   or   but

4.18

SKILLS

PAGE 26

**Mulder has lost sight of the monster. Copy and finish the
compound sentences below.**

> **1** Mulder decided to go back to his hotel **but** ...
>
> **2** He could hardly see the path **and** ...
>
> **3** He heard a snarling noise **but** ...
>
> **4** It might have been an alien **or** it could ...
>
> **5** He could go back to the hotel **or** he could ...
>
> **6** He saw the hotel lights shining in the distance **and** ...

Complex sentences

4.19

First read through these sentences.

1 Mulder, who was a special agent, enjoyed looking for UFOs and aliens.

2 Although Scully was his partner, she did not believe in UFOs and aliens.

3 They had great fun when they were sent out on a case.

4 Because he knew she wanted to find the truth, Mulder always took Scully with him.

5 Whenever the other agents heard about their work, they thought it was strange.

The sentences above are all **complex sentences**. Complex sentences have two different types of clauses:

a **main clause** which makes sense on its own:
Mulder enjoyed looking for UFOs and aliens.

and a **subordinate clause** which does not make sense on its own. It needs to be joined to a main clause to make sense:
who was a special agent

4.20

TRF
PAGE 26

Now divide each of the sentences at the top of the page into two clauses. Write them down.

2 a)   Although Scully was his partner
   b)   she did not believe in UFOs and aliens.

4.21

Look at each clause you found above. Write down whether it is a main clause or a subordinate clause.

4.22

Copy out the sentences below. Then underline the subordinate clauses.

1   When Mulder arrived, Scully told him about the monster.

2   The monster, who had been hiding, was hungry.

3   It jumped out at Mulder when he opened the door.

4   Scully reached for her gun, which was loaded.

5   After she fired, the monster slithered onto the floor.

TRF
PAGE 23

Commas are sometimes needed to separate the subordinate clause from the main clause so that the sentence makes sense.

4.23

SKILLS
PAGE 27

Match one subordinate clause to each main clause and make five complex sentences. Write them out.

Main clauses	Subordinate clauses
1 Mulder was yelling	a) if it was captured alive.
2 He was very upset	b) because it was lying so still.
3 The monster looked dead	c) after the monster groaned.
4 The monster could help them	d) although he had not been shot.
5 Mulder felt much happier	e) which surprised Scully.

When you are writing, remember to use a mixture of simple, compound and complex sentences. This will make your writing more interesting to read.

UNIT
5 The past is present

5.1

Read the passage opposite. Then answer the questions below.
Mrs Harris is eighty-seven. She lives with her son Henry's family.

5.2

Work in pairs. Find parts of the text that show that:

1 Mrs Harris has problems walking.

2 She has no sense of what time it is.

3 She does not know what to wear to go shopping.

4 She cannot make use of important information.

5.3

Work in a group. List eight worries Henry might have because his mother is like this.

Mrs Harris might ...   She could go out ...   People might ...

5.4

TRF
PAGE 28
SEE ALSO
PAGES 52–53

Imagine you are a social worker. You think that Mrs Harris needs the care of an old people's home. Write a report explaining:

1 What is unusual and risky about Mrs Harris' behaviour.

2 What might happen to Mrs Harris because she is like this.

3 What could be done for her.

REPORT – Mrs A. Harris aged 87
Mrs Harris lives with ... Recently her behaviour has ...

Flowers for Harry Rowe

As Henry Harris carried the six empty milk bottles along the hall that night, he bumped into his mother, who was shuffling slowly backwards out of her room.

5 Mrs Harris smiled with delight at meeting her son so unexpectedly. She wore a cast-off dressing-gown of Henry's, tied loosely with a flower patterned belt from one of her best Oxfam dresses. Upon her feet were Henry's bedroom slippers held in place by wide brown elastic bands dropped on the doorstep by the postman. The morning newspaper was clamped
10 under her arm, and on her head she wore a badly **moulting** feather hat that dated from before the war.

'Hello there, Mum,' said Henry Harris. 'What are you up to at this time of night?'

Mrs Harris rooted anxiously inside her purse.

15 'I'm off to buy a **wreath** for Harry Rowe,' she confided.

'He's not dead yet.'

'I'll put all your names on the card as well.'

'But he's not *dead*.'

'I'll get a good one.' Mrs Harris delved some more among
20 her loose coins. 'About fifteen **shillings**?'

'Not a wreath, Mum. Perhaps some flowers. I suppose there's a faint chance he might be feeling a little unwell ...'

'I prefer a *wreath*, Henry. I'll choose a nice one.'

Henry looked out of the front door into the pitch black
25 night. He wondered momentarily whether to open battle on another front – the fact that the florist closed several hours ago – and then decided not to bother.

'You can't send Harry Rowe a wreath while he's *alive*.'

30 'Perhaps a nice one in the shape of a cross?'

'I'll get it.'

And Henry, sighing heavily, tucked two of the milk bottles under his left arm, slid a third on to a spare little finger, and held out his free hand. Mrs Harris, pleased and relieved, handed her
35 bead purse over to him, and shuffled back inside her room.

Adapted from *The Granny Project* by Anne Fine

> **moulting** – losing its feathers
> **wreath** – flowers for someone who has died
> **shillings** – old coins

5.5 Jack and Jean Atkinson (both 72) love going clubbing. They appeared on BBC1's *Here and Now* programme. Read the transcript (the words actually spoken) opposite.

5.6 Work in pairs. Read the report below. Note down at least four ways in which the report and film transcript are different.

Here and Now showed a film report about Jack and Jean Atkinson's unusual hobby. The elderly couple have spent 636 evenings in night clubs during the last three years.
Viewers were shown the couple drinking champagne. They
5 challenged the younger reporter Wendy to keep up with them. They wanted to show 'they are made of strong stuff'.
   At the night club Jack and Jean danced continually. Wendy became tired after 2am and stopped dancing. The film report ended with Jack and Jean still dancing at 3am. The disc jockey
10 told them it was the last dance of the evening.

5.7 Match and compare the spoken language of the film with the written language that is saying the same thing. For example: 1 = c

Spoken language (film transcript)

1 **Incomplete sentences:** Last one ... (line 35)

2 **Informal English:** wrinkly ravers. (line 19)

3 **Pauses:** I agreed to hit the high life with the groovy geriatrics ... Cheers everybody! (lines 9–11)

4 **Abbreviations:** they're (line 3) OK. (line 24)

5 **Padding phrases:** I admit it – I'm flagging. (line 24)

6 **Present tense:** Let's hope you can keep up with us tonight, Wendy. (lines 12–13)

Written language (report)

A **No abbreviations:** 'they are made of strong stuff.' (line 6)

B **Past tense:** They challenged the younger reporter Wendy to keep up with them. (lines 4–5)

C **Complete sentences:** The disc jockey told them it was the last dance of the evening. (lines 9–10)

D **No padding phrases:** Wendy became tired after 2 am and stopped dancing. (lines 7–8)

E **No pauses – formal sentences and punctuation:** viewers were shown the couple drinking champagne. (line 4)

F **Formal English:** elderly couple. (line 2)

Jack and Jean are dressing up in their club gear.

COMMENTATOR: While most old folk are ready to drop off – in this house they're ready to bop! And boy, do this couple party! They go clubbing four nights a week! Yet she gets a pension and he's got a bus pass.

Wendy, Jean and Jack are sipping champagne.

WENDY: No spring chicken myself, I agreed to hit the high life with the groovy **geriatrics** ... Cheers, everybody!

JACK: Let's hope you can keep up with us tonight, Wendy.

WENDY: You just try me!

15 *Wendy, Jean and Jack are at the disco.*

COMMENTATOR: It's midnight and the 636th time Jack and Jean have stepped out in Huddersfield in under three years. Here come the wrinkly ravers – let's see what they're made of ...

Jack and Jean are dancing.

DJ: Jack and Jean are moving well ...

Later – Wendy is dancing but looking tired.

WENDY: OK – I admit it – I'm flagging ... I've lost count of how many times I've danced round my handbag. It's past 2am in Huddersfield and I'm worn out by the crumbly clubbers. I can't take much more of this!

Later still.

COMMENTATOR: Nor can the DJ. It's 3am!

DJ: Really, Jack and Jean – this has to be the last one – I want to go home, OK? Last one ...

JACK & JEAN: Oh no, no ...

geriatrics – old people

5.8

Read the poem opposite. In pairs, think of three possible titles for this poem. Choose the best. Be ready to explain to your class why it is the best.

5.9

Work on your own.

1 Read stanza 1. What did the poet like about visiting his grandfather?

2 Read stanza 2. Why was it rude to say 'Put it out yourself'?

3 Read stanza 3. Then find:
a) two words or phrases that show that grand-dad is old.
b) four words or phrases showing how angry grand-dad is.

4 Read stanza 4. Which words make the ash hole seem scary?

5 How have the boy's feelings towards seeing his grandfather changed in stanza 5? Why is this?

5.10

SKILLS

PAGES 30–31

The mother asks her son why he has stopped visiting his grand-dad. Write his *truthful* answer. He should explain *without copying the poem*:

1 What he did wrong.

2 What grand-dad did to him.

3 Why he might be scared to go back.

4 What he might miss about going to his grand-dad's house.

I was at grand-dad's house one day and he asked me to ...
I know it was rude but I was busy ... and ...

1   I always liked my grand-dad's house,
With the white fungus in the cellar,
Narrow winding stairs up to the attic,
And the amazing maze of kitchens,
Corridors, **sculleries**, the sheds.

2   Until one day, I cheeked him to his face.
He said quite simply, 'Put the dog out, lad.'
But I was busy exploring a drawer
And said, 'Put it out yourself.'

3   A moment of shocked silence hung in the air,
And then the old man roared.
He coughed and spluttered, staggered,
And grabbed me by the neck.
His horny nails bit into my flesh.
'Any more lip from you, my lad,
And I'll chuck you down **th'ess'ole**.'

4   Meaning the hole for ash beneath the fire,
A hole that glowed bright red like hell,
And seemed to breathe in every draught.

5   For months, whenever I was bored on rainy days,
And Mother said, 'Go and see your grand-dad,'
Suddenly, as if by magic, I'd find lots of things to do
So that I needn't face the jaws of hell.

By Geoffrey Summerfield

sculleries – rooms where the dishes were washed
th'ess'ole – a dialect word meaning the hole under
the grate which the ashes from the fire fall into

49

Agreement of subject and verb

Remember that the **subject** is the person or thing doing the verb. Look at this sentence:

They walk to the nightclub.

To find the subject:

1 Find the verb – *walk*

2 Ask: 'Who or what *walk*?' Answer: *They walk.*

They is the subject of the sentence.

5.11

Copy out the sentences below. Circle the verb. Underline the subject.

1 I walk to the nightclub.

2 You walk to my house.

3 He walks to the same nightclub.

4 She walks with him.

5 It walks behind them.

6 We walk back together.

7 They walk back later.

Notice that the way the verb is written changes depending on the *person* and *number* of the subject.

1 The way the verb is written has to *agree* with the *person* doing the verb, for example:

I walk   *but*   **he** walks
(1st person)   (3rd person)

2 The way the verb is written also has to agree with the number of people doing the verb, for example:

he walks   *but*   **they** walk
(one person)   (more than one person)

Always check your own writing. Write the verb in a way that *agrees* with the subject.

5.12

The table below shows the *agreement* of subject and verbs that are used often. It shows how they change depending upon *person* and *number*. Read it and use it to help you with the activities below.

Subject	Verb				
I	go/**am** going	make/**was** making	take/**have** taken	say	like
you	go/**are** going	make/**were** making	take/**have** taken	say	like
he/she/it	goes/**is** going	makes/**was** making	takes/**has** taken	says	likes
we	go/**are** going	make/**were** making	take/**have** taken	say	like
they	go/**are** going	make/**were** making	take/**have** taken	say	like

5.13

Rewrite the sentences below. Change the verbs in bold so that they *agree* with the subject. Look back at the table to help you.

1 I **goes** to 'The Vibes' every Saturday.

2 I **likes** it best when you come with me.

3 We **makes** a good couple when we dance together.

4 They **says** we make a great team.

5.14

TRF
PAGE 29
SKILLS
PAGE 32

Rewrite the paragraph below. Change the verbs in bold so that they *agree* with the subject. The table above will help you.

On Saturdays we **goes** to the sports centre. They **has** lots of things you can do there. We **likes** going for a drink in the café. Last week they **was** making some changes. It **were** really noisy and messy. But now we **has** a computer room to go in, too. I **says** it's brilliant! Afterwards you **comes** home with me and we **gets** a video out.

Formal and informal English

5.15

Read the passages below.

A

'I remember hiding under our dining table with my mother. There wasn't time to get into the air raid shelter. There was one tremendous bang and then another as two bombs landed near our house. The glass in our windows was blown in and the ceilings crashed down around us. It's amazing we survived.'

B

Mrs Johnson and her son Matthew were hiding beneath their dining table when the two bombs exploded. They had been unable to reach the air raid shelter in time. Only the windows and ceilings were damaged in their house.

5.16

Now answer the questions.

1 Write down the facts in A.

2 Do the same facts appear in B?

3 Which passage is written in more formal language?

4 Which passage is written in the first person and which in the third person?

Sometimes you may be asked to turn some notes or someone's words into a **report** like passage B.

A report gives information to an important person or group.

A report is a formal piece of writing. It is written:

1 In the third person: *their house* instead of *my house*.

2 As if the writer does not know the people in the report: *Mrs Johnson and her son Matthew...* instead of *I remember ...*

3 In Standard English without slang or dialect words: *were damaged* instead of *was blown in*.

5.17

Rewrite the passage below. Change it from first person to third person.

> I heard someone calling for help. My neighbour, Mrs Bradley, was lying underneath some rubble. I told her not to panic and I ran to get my mother. We both tried to free her but it seemed to take forever.
>
> Matthew heard someone calling for help. His neighbour ...

5.18

SKILLS
PAGE 33

Rewrite these sentences, changing the words in bold to formal ones. Use words from the box below.

> 1 I was **scared stiff** when the bombs went off.
>
> 2 Mrs Bradley was **as fit as a fiddle** until she had her accident.
>
> 3 I **shot off** to get some help.
>
> 4 It took us **ages and ages** to get the rubble off Mrs Bradley.
>
> 5 We were **shattered to bits** when we finally freed her.

> hurried   frightened   a long time   healthy   tired

5.19

TRF
PAGE 30

Matthew has to write a report to tell the War Office what happened. Rewrite his speech as a report.

> I was shaking like a leaf when the ceiling crashed in. The noise of the bricks smashing down made a right racket. I thought my time was up. My mum was as white as a sheet. We raced outside to see what had happened to the rest of the street. I could see Mrs Bradley trapped under a load of rubble. She was panicking like mad. We finally got her free. Some neighbours gave us a hand to carry her to safety.

UNIT 6 It's a strange world!

6.1 Read the passage opposite. It is from a science fiction story set in the future. Leonard Mead is out walking when a police car stops him.

6.2 Answer the questions below. Say which parts of the text show your answers are right.

1 Read lines 1–11. Why was Leonard out walking?

2 Read lines 12–23. Why does the police car think Leonard does not need to walk? How do you know the police car disapproves of walking?

3 How do most people in the story spend their evenings? What does Leonard think about living like that?

4 Read lines 24–41. Who arrested Leonard Mead? Why do you think he was taken to a hospital?

6.3 Work in a group. Think of science fiction books, programmes or films you have seen. Make a list of the kind of things that happen in science fiction (its features).

aliens ... takes place in the future ... bugs ... no freedom

6.4

TRF
PAGE 32
SKILLS
PAGE 34

Leonard sees four of the features you noted above during his journey to the hospital. Write about his journey. Describe what he sees in detail.

As the police car sped along Leonard stared out of the window. A video on the outside of each front door showed what the people inside were doing ...

Just walking!

'Your name?' said the police car. Leonard couldn't see the men in it for the bright light in his eyes.

'Leonard Mead,' he said.

The machine-like voice hissed, 'What are you doing out?'

5 'Walking,' said Leonard Mead.

'Walking!'

'Just walking,' he said simply, but his face felt cold.

'Walking, just walking, walking?'

'Yes, sir.'

10 'Walking where? For what?'

'Walking for air. Walking to *see*.'

'Your address?'

'Eleven South Saint James Street.'

'There is air *in* your house, you have an air *conditioner*?'

15 'Yes.'

'And you have a viewing screen in your house to see with?' the voice said.

'No,' Leonard said.

'No? Have you done this *walking* often, Mr Mead?'

20 'Every night for years.'

Everything went on in the tomb-like houses at night now, Leonard thought. The tombs, ill-lit by television light, where the people sat like the dead.

The police car sat in the centre of the street with its radio
25 throat faintly humming.

'Well, Mr Mead,' it said. 'Here.' There was a sigh, a pop. The door of the police car sprang wide. 'Get in.'

'Wait a minute, I haven't done anything!'

'Get in.'

30 Leonard walked like a man suddenly drunk. As he passed the front window of the car he looked in. As he had expected, there was no one in the front seat, no one in the car at all. He put his hand to the door and peered into the back seat, which was a little cell, a little black jail with bars.

35 'Where are you taking me?'

The car hesitated, or rather gave a faint whirring click, 'To the **Psychiatric Centre for Research**.'

He got in. The door shut with a soft thud.

40 The police car rolled through the night avenues, flashing its dim lights, and took him away.

Adapted from *The Pedestrian* by Ray Bradbury

Psychiatric Centre for Research – a hospital where people are taken to have their minds and the way they think examined

6.5 Read the passage opposite. Maria and Dag are writing about their travels in Vietnam. Their guide, Binh, has brought them to his friend Chin's restaurant.

6.6 Work in pairs. Read lines 7–19. How would you feel about holding this snake? Would you eat it?

6.7 Work in pairs. Copy and complete the chart below.

Character	Lines	How the person reacts to the snake
Chin	7–10, 13	Chin is used to handling snakes; he …
Binh	11–12	Binh says … but has pushed … so he must feel …
	16–18	Binh has moved even … so he must feel …
	23–24	Now the snake is …. Binh is …
Dag	13–15, 19–20	Dag isn't … even when … He says …
Maria	14, 25–30	Maria is worried when … When she sees … She decides to …

6.8

TRF
PAGE 33
SKILLS
PAGE 35

Maria is describing a new experience. She is seeing a different way of life and of eating. How has she made it entertaining? How has she helped the reader see what happened through her eyes?

Use your chart to help you write about how Maria describes:

1 entering the restaurant, seeing the snake and what the snake does

2 Binh's reaction to the live snake

3 Dag and Chin's reaction to the live snake

4 why Maria decides to order an omelette.

Snake Curry

Quickly, we clambered up the steep river bank and into a restaurant that overlooked the water. On a counter top near the doorway was a **demi-john** filled with a clear liquid and several fat snakes curled up like lengths of rope.

5   'Chin wants to know which snake you like to eat,' Binh said.

    'Cobra's her favourite,' joked Dag.

    Chin came out of the kitchen. Instead of a towel around his neck he had a snake. It was about **three feet** long. It had a brown back and cream and black striped belly. Chin placed it on the table, holding its

10 tail. It slithered across towards me, its tongue flickering in and out.

    'He say it no poisonous,' said Binh, who had pushed his chair to a safe distance from the table.

    Chin picked up the writhing snake and placed it on Dag's knees.

    'For God's sake don't let it go up your shorts!' I cried.

15   Coolly, Dag picked it up by the base of its head.

    'He say price of snake is 35 000 dong,' called Binh, who was now halfway across the room. 'He cook it with the vegetable and spice and hot chilli.'

    'Good deal,' said Dag, carefully examining the snake. 'We'll take it.'

20   'I've always liked snakes,' said Dag, ten minutes later.

    This was just as well because he was about to eat one. The creature had been killed, chopped into chunks, fried, and covered in a thick sauce.

    'You try, very delicious,' said Binh, who had pulled his chair back to the table.

25   'I'm forever amazed at what you'll put in your mouth,' I said, as a chunk of flesh disappeared into Dag's mouth.

    Half a minute later, some rather surprising things came out. First a large piece of bone, then some skin that he'd sucked clean of sauce. I could see the cream and black markings and the scales.

30   Catching Chin's eye, I ordered an omelette.

Adapted from *Three Moons in Vietnam* by Maria Coffey

demi-john – large glass jar
three feet – about one metre

6.9 | Read the poem opposite. Then answer the questions below.

6.10 | Poets often make us look at familiar objects in a different way. Read the five highlighted images (A–E) in the poem. Match them to the pictures.

6.11 | Decide whether the feeling about the moon is pleasant or mysterious in each of the five stanzas. Copy and complete the chart below to show why this is.

Stanza	Feeling	Words creating that feeling	Pictures these words create (effect)
1	pleasant	gently bouncing ... vast balloon	This stanza makes the moon sound like a beautiful hot air balloon or a child's balloon floating in the breeze.
2		booming softly ... like a bassoon	The moon sounds like ...
3	mysterious	A kneeling vigil, in a religious hush.	It is as if the trees are worshipping the ...
4			

6.12
TRF
PAGE 34
| Think of six images you could use to describe the sun. Three should be pleasant and three unpleasant. Use the diagram below to help you.

6.13 | Now write a description of a summer's day at the beach. It does not have to be a poem. Make the feeling about the sun change from pleasant to unpleasant.

> We got up early just as the sun was rising like a ... . When we arrived at the beach the sun smiled on us with a warm ...

The Harvest Moon

1　The flame-red moon, the harvest moon,
　Rolls along the hills, gently bouncing,
　A vast balloon,　　　　　　　　　　　　　　A
　Till it takes off, and sinks upward
　To lie in the bottom of the sky, like a gold **doubloon**.　B

2　The harvest moon has come,
　Booming softly through heaven, like a **bassoon**.　C
　And earth replies all night, like a deep drum.

3　So people can't sleep,
　So they go out where elms and oak trees keep　D
　A kneeling **vigil**, in a religious hush.
　The harvest moon has come!

4　And all the moonlit cows and all the sheep
　Stare up, **petrified**, while the moon swells
　Filling heaven, as if red hot, and sailing　　　E
　Closer and closer like the end of the world.

5　Till the gold fields of stiff wheat
　Cry 'We are ripe, reap us!' and the rivers
　Sweat from the melting hills.

By Ted Hughes

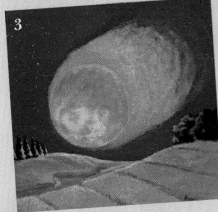

> **doubloon** – an old gold coin
>
> **bassoon** – a musical instrument you blow.
> It makes a deep, low sound.
>
> **vigil** – time spent awake watching or praying
>
> **petrified** – the animals are so frightened they
> cannot move

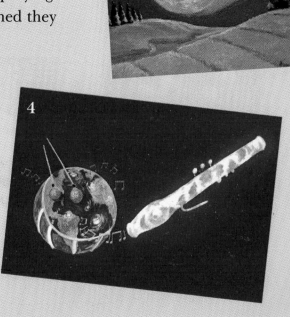

Imagery: similes and metaphors

Imagery is a type of description. An **image** is a group of words that make a picture to show what something is like.

There are two main sorts of imagery:

1 **simile** where two things are compared (said to be like each other). The writer uses the words **as** or **like**:

*The moon is **like** a gold doubloon.*   *The moon is as red **as** flame.*

2 **metaphor** where two things are compared but this time the writer does *not* use the words **as** or **like**. It *is* the other thing:
*The moon **is** a vast balloon.*

6.14

The sentences below describe a stormy day at the seaside. Say which images are similes and which are metaphors.

1 The sea roared like an angry lion.

2 The clouds were as dirty as grey rags.

3 The foaming waves were sharp white fangs.

4 Wind swept along the beach like an invisible hand.

6.15

Work in pairs. Which picture shows the stormy day described above? Explain how the images above help you to recognise it.

6.16

Write a short description for picture 2 above. Use similes and metaphors to make it interesting to read.

When you read an image:

The foaming waves were sharp white fangs.

you need to decide two things:

1 In what way the image is like the object being described.

   The white foam on the waves looks like sharp fangs/teeth.

2 How the image makes the object 'sound'. What picture does it create in your mind?

   The image makes you think the waves are dangerous, as if they have teeth like a vicious lion. They seem to be roaring and trying to eat everything in sight.

6.17

Copy and complete the chart below. Explain how each image is like the thing being described. Think about the picture the image brings to your mind.

Image	Why it is like the thing being described	The picture or feeling the image creates
The volcano roared like a raging dragon.	The volcano is breathing fire like a dragon. It's erupting.	The fire from the volcano is loud and hot. It sounds very dangerous and angry.
The bare branches clawed like witches' fingers at the moonlit sky.	The branches are long and thin. They look like the fingers of an old witch.	
Diamonds of white snow sparkled in the sun.		
Icicles hung in daggers across the frozen window pane.		
Raindrops tiptoed like delicate ballet dancers across the emerald green grass.		
Hail thundered across the roof like bullets from a machine gun.		

TRF
PAGE 35
SKILLS
PAGES 36–37

Use images in your own writing. They will make your descriptions more interesting and exciting to read.

Paragraphs: introductions and conclusions

A paragraph is a group of sentences written about the same topic. In any piece of writing these paragraphs do important jobs:

1 The **introduction** – the first paragraph tells the reader what the piece of writing is going to be about.

2 The **middle** paragraph(s) – these contain the main points.

3 The **conclusion** – the last paragraph brings the writing to a close.

Pieces of writing should always include an introduction, the main points you are making, and a conclusion.

6.18 Read and match the introductions and conclusions on the opposite page. There are three pieces of writing.

6.19

TRF
PAGE 36

Work in pairs. Read each introduction.

1 What *type* of writing is each one? How can you tell?

Paragraph A is the introduction to a letter complaining about a television set. It states clearly in the first sentence that ...

2 What clues does each introduction give you about what might come next?

In Paragraph A it says ... so you know that ...

6.20

SKILLS
PAGES 38–39

Write an introduction for the following pieces of writing.

1 A letter asking for two tickets to see your favourite group in concert at the NEC Birmingham.

2 A story called 'My Most Embarrassing Moment'.

3 A report on your favourite team's last match.

Introductions

A

I wish to complain about the television I bought from your shop on 23rd June. It was a colour Hitani 473 with a remote control. I expected it to have been tested for safety.

B

Mary Watkins, aged 95, was robbed of £100 on Wednesday, 3rd September. Two women pretending to be raising money for charity asked for a drink of water. When Mary went to fetch the drink she didn't realise how her kindness was going to be repaid.

C

My story begins one warm Sunday when my family and I were heading off to Devon. We packed the car early. Nobody argued over who sat in the front seat. The car didn't break down as we set off. It was going to be a perfect holiday. My mother had checked nobody was left behind. My father was smiling. How could anything go wrong?

Conclusions

D

At last our holiday had come to an end. I have never been so glad to see 44, Acorn Avenue! We piled out of the car and rushed up to the front door. Home at last!

E

The two women stole her handbag, which was hanging up in the hallway and contained £100. They were in their thirties, dressed in jeans and white T shirts. If you have any information please phone Aden Police on 4355432.

F

I should like you to replace the television and pay for the redecoration of my lounge which is needed after the fire caused by your faulty television.

7 Shakespeare's king killer

TRF
PAGE 38

Macbeth is a play about ambition, betraying friends and murder. It was written by William Shakespeare and was probably first performed in 1606. The play is set in Scotland in around 1040.

7.1

Read about the main characters in *Macbeth*. They are described as they appear at the beginning of the play.

Macbeth is the main character. He's a brave Scottish soldier. He leads the Scottish army alongside Banquo. At the beginning of the play they have just won a battle. Macbeth is a national hero. He is returning home.

Macbeth:
- brave in battle
- ambitious
- superstitious
- can be a weak person
- can easily be swayed
- can be cruel
- has a vivid imagination
- capable of murder

Lady Macbeth is Macbeth's wife. She is at home waiting for Macbeth to return from battle.

Lady Macbeth:
- loyal
- ambitious
- persuasive
- strong personality
- capable of planning murder
- cannot cope with guilt

Banquo leads the Scottish army along with Macbeth and is Macbeth's friend. He has a young son called Fleance. Banquo is on the way home with Macbeth.

Banquo:
- brave
- trustworthy
- caring father
- less ambitious than Macbeth
- not as superstitious as Macbeth

Duncan is King of Scotland. He is a good king who punishes traitors and rewards good soldiers. He is about to have a traitor called the Thane of Cawdor killed. He will then reward Macbeth by giving him the title Thane of Cawdor. (Thane means nobleman of Scotland.)

Duncan:
- good king
- honest
- trusts too easily

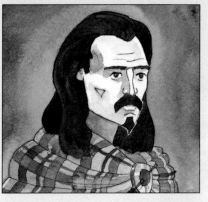

Malcolm is Duncan's son who eventually becomes King. Like his father, he believes in law and order. He rewards good people. Duncan is about to announce that Malcolm will follow him as King after his death.

Malcolm:
- believes in law and order
- rewards good people
- better judge of character and less trusting than his father Duncan

Macduff is a brave, loyal soldier who also fights in the Scottish army. He is loyal to his King and country. He is married with children.

Macduff:
- brave
- loyal
- wants to make sure Scotland is ruled well
- will take action
- a good leader

7.2

TRF

PAGE 39

Work in pairs. Work out a quiz about the different characters. Make up two questions about each character in turn. Try out your quiz on another pair.

Read about what happens in *Macbeth*.

1 Macbeth and Banquo are riding home from winning a battle. Three witches lie in wait for them. They say:

> Macbeth, you'll be Thane of Cawdor.

> Then you'll become King of Scotland.

> Banquo, your descendants will be kings.

2 Then messengers arrive with news.

> Macbeth, King Duncan has put the Thane of Cawdor to death as he was a traitor. You are now Thane of Cawdor as a reward for your bravery.

3 Banquo and Macbeth are shocked. The witches' words have come true.

> Those witches are up to no good.

> The witches were right in what they said. Maybe I'll be King, too!

4 An announcement is made.

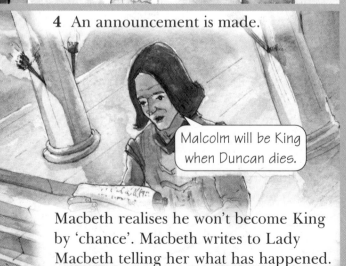

> Malcolm will be King when Duncan dies.

Macbeth realises he won't become King by 'chance'. Macbeth writes to Lady Macbeth telling her what has happened.

5 Duncan comes to stay at Macbeth's castle. Lady Macbeth welcomes him – but she has an evil plan.

> We can murder Duncan while he's here. Then Macbeth might be King. But Macbeth might not go through with it. Spirits – make me cruel to help him.

6 Macbeth feels uneasy about killing Duncan. Lady Macbeth needs to persuade him.

You're such a coward!

I'm not – I'm a real man. I'll prove it to you and kill him.

7 Macbeth stabs King Duncan while he is asleep. Then he is terrified.

Oh no, what have I done?

Pull yourself together! Give me those daggers. I'll wipe the blood on Duncan's servants while they're asleep. They'll get the blame.

8 Macduff discovers Duncan and shouts for help. Macbeth comes running.

Help! Murder!

The servants did it – they're covered in blood. I'll kill them!

9 Duncan's sons are afraid for their lives. They run away. Macbeth is crowned King.

10 Banquo is suspicious.

Did Macbeth murder Duncan?

Macbeth remembers the witches saying Banquo's descendants will be kings. So he has Banquo murdered but Banquo's son Fleance escapes.

11 Then Macbeth's first state banquet is ruined.

Banquo's ghost has come to haunt me! What have I done?

Macbeth's so scared he'll give the game away! I'd better say he's ill and ask the guests to leave …

12 Macbeth is afraid. He asks the witches to tell him the future. They show him:

a A head in armour

b A child covered in blood

c A child carrying a tree

d Banquo's descendants as kings

Beware Macduff.

None of woman born shall harm Macbeth.

Macbeth shall never vanquished be Until Great Birnam Wood to high Dunsinane Hill Shall come against him.

Macbeth thinks no one can harm him because of what the witches show him. But he still has Macduff's family killed. Macduff had already gone to England to join Malcolm. When Macduff hears the news he wants revenge. Malcolm and Macduff's army set off to fight Macbeth.

13 Back in Scotland, guilty Lady Macbeth is sleepwalking. A doctor is called to help her. She gives away her secrets.

Dead ... murdered ... Duncan, Banquo, Lady Macduff, ...

This isn't a matter for a doctor, it's a matter for a priest ...

14 Malcolm and Macduff bring an army to fight Macbeth. They carry branches from Birnam Wood so Macbeth cannot see how many of them are coming. The witches' words are coming true.

15 News arrives: Lady Macbeth is dead. Has she killed herself? Then battle begins and rages fiercely. Macduff fights and kills Macbeth.

You won't win. The witches said no man of woman born can hurt me.

But I was taken from my mother's womb before I could be born. Take that, Macbeth!

16 Malcolm is crowned King.

Now I can make Scotland safe again.

Finish the following sentences about the play *Macbeth*.

Pictures 1–5

1 Macbeth and ... are riding home from winning a battle when they meet ...

2 The witches promise Macbeth that ... They promise Banquo that ...

3 Their first promise comes true when ...

4 Then it is announced that ... will be King when Duncan dies. Macbeth realises if he wants to become King he ...

5 Lady Macbeth thinks ... might be too ... to kill Duncan so she ...

Pictures 6–11

6 ... works hard to persuade Macbeth to go ahead and kill Duncan. They carry out their plan and ...

7 Macbeth becomes King and Duncan's sons ...

8 Macbeth arranges for Banquo to be ... but ... escapes. Then at his first state banquet he sees Banquo's ...

Pictures 12–16

9 Macbeth sees the witches again who tell him that ...

10 Macbeth thinks the witches' words mean no one can ...

11 Macbeth is worried about Macduff so ... But Macduff has gone to England to ...

12 Meanwhile, Lady Macbeth feels ... and is ...

13 Macbeth discovers he has been wrong. Birnam Wood can ... because ... Macbeth can be killed because ...

14 At the end of the play both Macbeth and Lady Macbeth are ...

15 Malcolm is ... and Scotland is ...

7.5 **Work in pairs. How well does each description below match the play of *Macbeth*? Give reasons for your answers.**

exciting	romantic	mysterious	violent	action-packed
relaxing	surprising	funny	creepy	about good and evil

7.6   Read Macbeth's speech from Act 1 on the opposite page.

7.7   Work in pairs. Look at the sentences in today's English under the speech.

1   Match each sentence with the right part of the speech.

sentence 5 = A

2   Write out the sentences in today's English in the right order.

7.8   Copy and complete the chart below. Show Macbeth's arguments for and against killing Duncan.

For killing Duncan	Against killing Duncan
I am ambitious ...	I am his relative and ...

7.9   Choose the three words below that best describe Macbeth's character in this speech. Explain why each one suits him. Use quotations from the passage to support your answer.

ambitious	loyal	kind	unsure
fearful	calm	cruel	happy

7.10

TRF
PAGE 41
SKILLS
PAGES 42–43

You are going to talk to an actor who is about to play Macbeth. Make notes on the following.

1   What kind of person is Macbeth supposed to be?

Macbeth is ambitious and ...

2   How might the actor behave during this speech?

The actor might be unsure when he says ...

Macbeth has been told by witches that he will be King. He and Lady Macbeth have planned to kill King Duncan so that this can come true. Macbeth is trying to make up his mind. Should he go ahead with their plan to kill Duncan or not?

Shall I or shan't I?

A
If it were done, when 'tis done, then 'twere well
It were done quickly... that but this blow
Might be the be-all and the end-all ...

B
But in these cases
5   We still have judgement here, that we but teach
Bloody instructions, which being taught return
To plague th'inventor. This even-handed justice
Commends th'ingredients of our poisoned chalice
10   To our own lips.

C
He's here in double trust:
First, I am his kinsman and his subject,
Strong both against the deed; then, as his host,
Who should against his murderer shut the door,
15   Not bear the knife myself.

D
Besides, this Duncan
Hath borne his faculties so meek, hath been
So clear in his great office, that his virtues
Will plead like angels, trumpet-tongued against
The deep damnation of his taking-off.

E
20   ... I have no spur
To prick the sides of my intent, but only
Vaulting ambition, which o'erleaps itself,
And falls on th'other.

Adapted from *Macbeth* by William Shakespeare, Act 1 Scene 7

The same ideas in today's English

1   But I am spurred on by my strong ambition to be King.

2   But in this case if I'm found out I'll be killed.

3   There are strong things against it. First, he trusts me: I'm his relative and his subject. Also I'm his host. I ought to protect him, not murder him.

4   Besides, this Duncan is a gentle man and a great King. He doesn't deserve to be murdered.

5   If I could murder Duncan and be certain of getting away with it, I would kill him quickly.

7.11 Lady Macbeth thinks Macbeth should kill Duncan while he is staying with them. Read their speeches opposite.

7.12 Work in pairs. Read lines 1–21. Match the sentences below to the right lines in the scene. Then write out the sentences below in the right order. *Sentence 3 = A*

Macbeth	**1** If we fail, what will happen then?
Lady Macbeth	**2** Were you a beast when you told me your idea, then?
Macbeth	**3** I dare do anything a real man would do. Anyone who dares to do more is not a real man.
Lady Macbeth	**4** If you pluck up your courage we won't fail.
Lady Macbeth	**5** When you dared do it – that's when you were a real man.
Lady Macbeth	**6** I would rather kill my own baby than behave like you!
Lady Macbeth	**7** Now the time and place are right, you can't go through with it.

7.13 Read lines 22–36. Match the pictures below to the right parts of the speeches. Then write a caption for each picture to explain in your own words how Macbeth and his wife will murder the king.

A

B

C

7.14 Write notes for an actor who is going to play Lady Macbeth. Describe her character. Start by explaining how she is:

TRF
PAGE 42
SKILLS
PAGES 44–45

strong	pushy	sure of what she wants	hard	clever

Lady Macbeth knows Macbeth is not sure about killing Duncan. She is ambitious and tries to persuade Macbeth to go ahead. She says if he does not then he is not a man but a coward ...

Go on, you coward!

MACBETH:	I dare do all that may become a man; Who dares do more, is none.	A
LADY MACBETH:	What beast was't then That made you first break this enterprise to me?	B
5	When you durst do it, then you were a man; And to be more than what you were, you would Be so much more the man.	C
	Nor time nor place Did then adhere, and yet you would make both. 10 They have made themselves, and that their fitness now Does unmake you.	D
	I have given suck, and know How tender 'tis to love the babe that milks me – I would, while it was smiling in my face, 15 Have plucked my nipple from his boneless gums, And dashed the brains out, had I so sworn as you Have done to this.	E
MACBETH:	If we should fail?	F
LADY MACBETH:	We fail? 20 But screw your courage to the sticking-place, And we'll not fail:	G
	when Duncan is asleep – Whereto the rather shall his day's hard journey Soundly invite him – his two chamberlains 25 Will I with wine and wassail convince ... What cannot you and I perform upon Th'unguarded Duncan? What not put upon His spongy officers, who shall bear the guilt Of our great quell?	
30 **MACBETH:**	... Will it not be receiv'd When we have mark'd with blood those sleepy two Of his own chamber, and used their very daggers, That they have done't?	
LADY MACBETH:	Who dares receive it other, 35 As we shall make our griefs and clamours roar, Upon his death?	

Adapted from *Macbeth* by William Shakespeare, Act 1 Scene 7

7.15

Macbeth goes ahead with the plan and kills Duncan. Lady Macbeth is waiting for him. Read opposite what happens next.

7.16

SKILLS
PAGES 46–47

Now answer the following questions. Use quotations from the text to show why your answers are right.

1 Read lines 1–7. How does Macbeth feel after killing Duncan?

   Macbeth feels ... He says 'This is a sorry ...' and 'Macbeth shall ...'

2 Read lines 8–11. What does Lady Macbeth think of Macbeth's worries?

3 Read lines 12–21. Why does Lady Macbeth take the daggers back? What will she use them for?

4 Read lines 23–31. How does Lady Macbeth think they can get rid of their guilt? What does Macbeth think?

7.17

Work in a group. Think about the murder of King Duncan. Who is the most guilty: Macbeth or Lady Macbeth? Give reasons.

7.18

TRF
PAGES 43–44
SKILLS
PAGES 48–49

Work in pairs. Look back at all your work on this play. Film director Stefan Zeelberg is making a film of *Macbeth*. He has asked for your help. You need to make notes on the following.

1 What is the play about? What would you say about the descriptions below?

   a) Greedy and over-ambitious people do terrible things.
   b) It's worth doing anything to get what you want.
   c) If you do something wrong you can get away with it.

2 What *type* of film do you think it would be? Romantic? Funny? Horrific? Tragic?

3 Which parts would be most exciting? Why?

4 What are the following characters like?

   a) Macbeth   *b)* Lady Macbeth   *c)* Duncan   *d)* Macduff.

5 Which actors would you choose to act the parts of:

   a) Macbeth   *b)* Lady Macbeth   *c)* Macduff?

Macbeth has just killed Duncan. He returns to Lady Macbeth with the daggers and blood on his hands. He is terrified about what he has done.

Murderers!

MACBETH:	I have done the deed ...
	This is a sorry sight.
	Looks on his hands
LADY MACBETH:	A foolish thought, to say a sorry sight ...
5 MACBETH:	Methought I heard a voice cry, 'Sleep no more!
	Macbeth does murder sleep'... and therefore ...
	Macbeth shall sleep no more.
LADY MACBETH:	Who was it, that thus cried? Why worthy Thane,
	You do unbend your noble strength, to think
10	So brainsickly of things. Go get some water,
	And wash this filthy witness from your hand.
	Why did you bring these daggers from the place?
	They must lie there. Go carry them, and smear
	The sleepy grooms with blood.
15 MACBETH:	I'll go no more
	I am afraid to think what I have done.
	Look on't again I dare not.
LADY MACBETH:	Infirm of purpose!
	Give me the daggers ... If he do bleed,
20	I'll gild the faces of the grooms withal,
	For it must seem their guilt.
	Exit. Knock within.
MACBETH:	Whence is that knocking?
	How ist with me, when every noise appals me? ...
25	Will all great Neptune's ocean wash this blood
	Clean from my hand? ...
LADY MACBETH:	My hands are of your colour; but I shame
	To wear a heart so white. [*Knock within*] I hear a knocking
	At the south entry. Retire we to our chamber.
30	A little water clears us of this deed ... Be not lost
	So poorly in your thoughts.
MACBETH:	To know my deed, 'twere best not know myself. [*Knock within*]
	Wake Duncan with thy knocking. I would thou couldst.

Adapted from *Macbeth* by William Shakespeare, Act 2 Scene 2

UNIT 8

Working on longer questions

This unit gives you practice at answering longer questions.

1 Read a longer question carefully.

2 Break it down into smaller parts. This makes it easier to answer. If there are bullet points they will guide you on what you might include in your answer. Make sure you write about each one.

3 Spend longer on questions that will give you more marks.

4 Use the skills you have learned to plan and write the best answer. Always remember three important things:

Point	+	**Comment**	+	**Evidence**
Make a point		Say how it answers the question		Support your answer with information from the text.

8.1 Read the passage opposite. Then read the questions below. The instructions are similar to those used on exam papers. The following pages will help you write a good answer.

Answer question 1 and question 2. Spend less time on question 1.

Refer to words and phrases in the passage to support each answer.

1 **What impression do you get of Kingshaw from the passage?**

In your answer you should comment on:
- the way Kingshaw reacts to the crow chasing him
- what happens to Kingshaw in the last two paragraphs.

2 **How does the writer build up a sense of fear and horror in this passage?**

In your answer you should comment on:
- the way the crow is described
- the effect the crow has on Kingshaw
- the way the writer uses sentence structure, vocabulary and punctuation.

This passage is about an eleven-year-old boy called Charles Kingshaw. He is being chased by a crow.

I'm the King of the Castle

When he first saw the crow he took no notice. There had been several crows. This one **glided** down into the corn on its enormous, ragged black wings. He began to be aware of it when it rose up suddenly. It circled
5 overhead, and then dived, to land not very far away from him. Kingshaw could see the feathers on its head, shining black in between the butter-coloured corn stalks. Then it rose, and circled, and came down again, this time not quite landing. It flapped about his head,
10 beating its wings and making a sound like flat leather pieces being slapped together. It was the largest crow he had ever seen. As it came down for the third time, he looked up and noticed its beak, opening in a screech. The inside of its mouth was scarlet, it had small
15 **glinting** eyes.

Kingshaw began to run, not caring if he trampled the corn, wanting to get away, down into the next field. He thought that the corn might be some kind of crow's food store in which he was seen as an **invader**. Perhaps this
20 was only the first of a whole **battalion** of crows that would rise up and swoop at him. Get on the grass then, he thought, get on to the grass, that'll be safe, it'll go away. He wondered if it had mistaken him for some **hostile** animal, lurking down in the corn.

25 Then, there was a single screech, and the terrible beating of wings, and the crow swooped down and landed in the middle of his back.

Kingshaw thought that, in the end, it must have been his screaming that frightened it off,
30 for he dared not move. He lay and closed his eyes and felt the claws of the bird, digging into his skin, through the thin shirt, and began to scream in a queer, gasping sort of way. After a moment or two, the bird rose. He had expected
35 it to begin pecking at him with his beak, remembering terrible stories about **vultures** that went for living people's eyes. He could not believe in his own escape.

Adapted from *I'm the King of the Castle* by Susan Hill

glided – flew without moving its wings

glinting – shining

invader – unfriendly intruder

battalion – large group

hostile – unfriendly

vultures – birds that eat human flesh

Before you begin to answer the questions make sure:

- you have **carefully read** the passage
- you **understand the questions** you are being asked
- you **know the main points** you need to make.

1 Some people underline the main parts of a question. This helps them remember what to cover in their answer.

2 Some people underline parts of the passage they will use in their answer. It helps them remember and refer to words and phrases which support their ideas.

8.2

Look again at question 1 on page 76, about your impressions of Kingshaw. What does each bullet point guide you to think about? Read the passage again. Jot down line numbers to use in your answer.

8.3

Work with a partner. Copy and complete the table below to help shape your answer.

Impressions of Kingshaw	My comment	Support
Kingshaw's reactions to the crow He's not scared to start with – it's only when the crow gets close that he gets frightened.	He seems like a normal boy. He's not easily scared, but the crow seems to be on the attack.	He only became aware of it when it 'rose up suddenly', circled overhead, then dived (lines 1–6).
He becomes more frightened as the crow gets closer.	The crow seems to be bullying Kingshaw. The description of the crow makes it sound evil. I'm not surprised Kingshaw is scared. I feel sorry for him.	(lines 6–15)
He thinks in a panicky way. You can tell his mind is racing with fear.		(lines 16–24)
What happens next?		
	It happens very quickly ...	(lines 25–27)
		(lines 28–38)

8.4

Now write your answer to question 1. Use the work you have done to help you.

8.5

Now carefully read through question 2 on page 76. Look at the first bullet point. How does the way the crow is described build up a sense of fear and horror? Read the statements below. Copy out the two that you think give the best answer.

1
The crow has big wings.

2
The crow is flying above Kingshaw and is quite close to him.

3
The crow has huge black wings which make it sound very scary. It is described as having 'enormous, ragged black wings'.

4
The crow seems to be chasing Kingshaw which is quite scary. It's almost as if it's trying to frighten him on purpose. The writer says: '... it rose up suddenly. It circled overhead, and then dived ...'

8.6

SEE ALSO
PAGE 92

Now write three other statements of your own. Look back at the passage. Quote from it to support your statements.

8.7

TRF
PAGE 46

Look at the second bullet point. How does Kingshaw's reaction to the crow build up a sense of fear and horror? Make notes about:

1 how fast Kingshaw runs   **2** the way he thinks

3 the noises he makes   **4** the way his imagination takes over.

8.8

Look at the third bullet point. With a partner, read the whole passage out loud. Make a note of:

1 where long sentences *and* short sentences are used, and why (e.g. lines 16–19, lines 1–3)

2 words or phrases which sound interesting, and why (e.g. line 7).

3 where lots of commas are used, and why (e.g. lines 21–23)

This part of your answer could start with something like:

The long sentences make it sound like things are happening in slow motion. The action lasts for quite a while.

8.9

SKILLS
PAGES 50–51

Now write your answer to question 2. Use the work you have done to help you.

You may be asked to read an advertisement and comment on how it persuades the reader. You may also be asked to look at the way it is presented (laid out). The work on the following pages will help you answer this kind of question.

8.10

TRF
PAGE 47

Read the advertisement opposite. Then read through the question below.

How does the advertisement persuade people to go on a cruise?

In your answer you should comment on:

1 two facts about cruises that the advertisement gives you

2 two words or phrases that would persuade readers to go on a cruise

3 how the advertisement is presented:
   - the use of photographs
   - the use of different types of print (e.g. bold, italic, capitals)
   - the layout

4 how effective you think the advertisement is.

8.11

Look at the first point. Decide which of the sentences below are facts. Note two facts from the text to use in your answer. Say *why* they might persuade you to go on the cruise.

1 Everything is plain sailing.

2 There are shops on board.

3 Every day will bring fresh surprises.

4 You can go to a fitness room on the cruise ship.

5 Chefs offer a variety of food on the ship.

Help

a fact is a piece of information which can be proved to be true:

Seaport Cruises organises coach and rail travel to the point of departure.

an opinion is someone's point of view: *Our menus are second to none.*

SEAPORT CRUISES
– for the trip of a lifetime

Waving goodbye to travel worries ...

Seaport Cruises offer an enjoyable and **convenient** way to travel. Our super service includes coach or rail connections to your **point of departure**. After that, everything is plain sailing. Once on board you can relax in style. Our comfortable cabins are **tailor-made** for all your holiday needs.

Holiday heaven ...

Every day will bring fresh surprises. Sailing with Seaport means you get the chance to take in stunning scenery and breathtaking beaches. The more adventurous can seek the sights and delights of charming cities, **traditional cultures** and bustling towns. The choice is yours – there really is something for everyone.

Let us entertain you ...

Evening entertainment is available every night. Our friendly staff will be on hand to make sure your stay with Seaport is as pleasurable as possible.

Shape up at our high-tech fitness suite which includes swimming pool, **sauna** and a range of exercise classes led by our fully trained instructors.

Shop till you drop in our top class stores or relax in one of our many bars and restaurants. Our top class chefs will tickle your taste buds with an amazing variety of food from other cultures. Our menus are second to none and offer a wide range of mouth-watering meals.

SEAPORT CRUISES
– taking the stress out of travel

convenient – easy to use
point of departure – where the ship leaves from
tailor-made – specially designed

traditional cultures – how people have lived for a long time
sauna – steam room

8.12

Look at the second point on page 80. Fill in a chart like the one below. List words and phrases that make cruising sound enjoyable. Say why they persuade you to go on the cruise.

Words and phrases	Reasons why they persuade you
everything is plain sailing	This suggests that things will go smoothly. You won't have to worry about things going wrong.
relax in style	The cruise sounds like a treat where everything you need will be supplied.
comfortable cabins	You will be comfortable. The cabins will be tailor-made for holiday needs, just right for ...

8.13

Now look at the third point on page 80. First brainstorm all the eye-catching things about each photograph. Think about:

1 the size of the photograph

2 where it appears on the page

3 the weather in the photograph

4 the colours used

5 the way people look

6 any other information about the cruise.

8.14

Now write a sentence about each of the points you have noticed. Say how they might persuade you to go on the cruise.

The photographs are quite large and are together so they catch your attention. The people look happy and relaxed. This would persuade you to go on the cruise because you imagine it is you sitting there, unwinding and enjoying yourself ...

8.15

Next make notes about the different types of print used in the advertisement. In each case say why each type might have been chosen. Think about:

1 The colours used: Do they attract your attention? Are they peaceful? Exciting?

2 The headings: why are they important?

3 The 'catchline' at the end. What is it trying to do?

8.16

Now look at the layout of the advertisement.

1 How many columns does it use? Is it easy to read?

2 Where is the heading? How does it attract your attention?

3 How is the text broken up? Does it keep you interested?

8.17

Now look at the fourth point on page 80. What would persuade you to go on the cruise? What would put you off? Is any important information missing from the advertisement? Fill in a table like the one below.

Good points	Bad points
It's good the way Seaport Cruises organises the transport so you don't have to waste time doing it yourself. You don't even have to worry about making your own way to the ship.	No price is given in the advertisement. You don't know if you're getting good value. It might cost £500 which is good. But it could cost over £2000 which might be too expensive.

8.18

SKILLS
PAGES 52–53

Now write your answer to the question. Make sure that you:

1 Use the work you have done to help answer each part of the question.

2 Write at least one paragraph about each point.

3 Refer to the text to support your answer.

4 Explain *how* the points you have made answer the question.

You may be asked to write a story, letter or advertisement. The work on the following pages will help you answer this kind of question.

8.19

Read through the questions below. Then answer the questions on the opposite page.

Choose **one** of the following:

Either

1   Write a story about being frightened. Try to build up a feeling of suspense.

Your story could be:
- a real-life incident that happened to you
- a description of a nightmare you have had
- something you wish to make up.

Or

2   Imagine you have returned from a disastrous holiday. Write a letter to the travel company. Complain about the things that happened.

In your letter you could write about:
- what you expected from the holiday
- what went wrong with the holiday
- what you expect the company to do about your complaint.

Write your address and today's date at the top of the letter. Begin your letter *Dear Sir or Madam.* End it with *Yours faithfully,* your signature and your printed name.

Or

3   The advertisement you read on page 81 tried to persuade people to travel with Seaport Cruises. Imagine you own a holiday company. Write an advertisement persuading people to go on the holiday of a lifetime. Decide where people are travelling to and how they will get there.

Think about:
- the layout of your advertisement
- the colour, pictures and types of print you might use to make it eye-catching
- the language you will use to persuade people to travel with you.

8.20 Always read questions and instructions carefully. Answer the following questions about the instructions on the opposite page.

1 How many questions do you need to answer?

2 Question 1: What must the story be about? What must you build up as you write the story?

3 Question 2: Who must you write to? What *sort* of letter is it?

4 Question 3: What must your advertisement try to do? How?

8.21 Look again at question 1 on page 84. Plan your story. Make notes.

1 Decide whether your story will be a real-life experience, a description of a nightmare or made up. What will it be about?

2 Decide who is in your story. Are you the only person or are there others? If so, who are they? What are they like? What can they see, hear, smell and touch? Why are they frightened?

3 Think about the setting for your story. Where does it take place? What time of year and day is it? What is the weather like?

4 You need to build up an atmosphere of fear and suspense. Jot down descriptive words and phrases you could use.

5 Plan a clear beginning, middle and end to your story.

8.22

SKILLS
PAGES 54–55

Now write your story. Make your writing interesting.

1 Use different *types* of sentences and start them in different ways.

2 Use a wide range of words.

3 Check your writing:

• Write in sentences. Each sentence should start with a capital letter and end with a full stop, question mark or exclamation mark.

• Break your work into parts or paragraphs.

• Check your work for spelling and punctuation errors.

8.23 Look at question 2 on page 84. What are you asked to write a letter about? What do the bullet points say you could include?

8.24 Look at the first bullet point. Brainstorm the things you would expect from a good holiday. Copy and complete the ideas below.

?		fresh bedding
good food		?
?		a good view
clean rooms		?

8.25 Look at the second bullet point. Brainstorm things that might go wrong with a holiday. Copy and complete the ideas below.

| ? | | ? |
| cockroaches | dirty bedding | ? | staff unfriendly and unhelpful |

8.26 Now look at the third bullet point. List the things you expect the travel company to do about your complaints.

1 Refund some or all of your money.   2 Offer you another ...

8.27

TRF
PAGE 48
SKIILLS
PAGES 56–57

Now write your letter. Use the work you have done to help you. Plan what to include in each paragraph. Remember to be polite.

1 Write your address and the date on the top right hand side. Start the letter *Dear Sir or Madam*.

2 Plan what to put in each paragraph:
- paragraph 1: say why you are writing
- paragraph 2: outline what you expected from your holiday
- paragraphs 3 and 4: explain what went wrong
- paragraph 5: say what you expect the company to do about it.

3 Finish your letter with *Yours faithfully*, your signature and your printed name.

8.28 Look at question 3 on page 84. What must your advertisement do? Look back at the advertisement for Seaport Cruises on page 80. Brainstorm what makes a good advertisement.

?

colourful photographs

GREECE

SOLD

good heading to attract attention

different types of print

?

?

8.29 Plan your own advertisement. Use the questions below to help you.

1 Decide where the holiday will be and how people will get there.

2 What interesting language will you use to persuade people to go on your holiday? If it is a holiday in the sun you might use words such as *relaxing, warm and welcoming, sun-drenched beaches*. Think up a good heading to start with.

3 What makes your holiday better than anyone else's? Will your advert include any special offers or money-off coupons?

4 Layout:
- how many columns will you use?
- how many paragraphs will you have? Why?
- where will your headings and pictures go? Why?

5 Colour, pictures and types of print:
- what colours will you use? Why?
- how many pictures will you have? What size will they be? Why?
- what different types and size of print will you use? Why?

8.30

TRF
PAGE 49
SKILLS
PAGES 58–59

Make a sketch of how you want your advertisement to look. This one might give you some ideas.

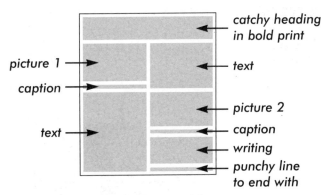

catchy heading in bold print

picture 1

text

caption

picture 2

text

caption

writing

punchy line to end with

8.31 Now write your advertisement. Include all your ideas. Break your work into paragraphs. Write in complete sentences.

Skills

Writing sentences correctly: revision

Remember that sentences must:

- make sense
- begin with a capital letter
- end with:

a full stop . a question mark ? or an exclamation mark !

9.1

Rewrite the following passage, breaking it into sentences. Put in the missing capital letters, full stops, question marks and exclamation marks.

it was Daniel's turn to have the barbecue in his garden his two friends, Jamie and Aysha, had come early to help him set up the barbecue 'where's your table' Aysha asked they helped him drag the big white table nearer the barbecue then they had to wash off all the garden chairs with the hose because they had got so dirty of course, Jamie couldn't resist trying to wash Danny off as well Danny had decided to put a purple streak in his hair for the party he wasn't too pleased when the colour ran 'is my face covered in purple now' Danny asked still, he got his own back later he put extra chilli sauce on Jamie's veggie burger

Using paragraphs and commas: revision

Remember to break your work into parts or **paragraphs**. This makes it easier to read. You often use paragraphs:

1 to break up a longer piece of writing

2 when you change the topic you are writing about to a new: *time*, *place*, *action*, *person*, *person speaking* or *idea*.

Remember to use **commas**:

1 To separate items in a list:
We took our passports, some warm clothes and a bag of food.

2 To show readers where to pause so that a sentence makes sense: *As we reached the harbour, people were waking up.*

3 Before opening speech marks, if the speech is part of a sentence: *I said, 'We're going fishing.'*

4 Before closing speech marks, if the speech is not a question or exclamation *and* is not at the end of the sentence: *'We're going train spotting,' said Midge.*

9.2

Rewrite the following passage so that it is correct. Add seven paragraphs and at least seven commas.

By the time we'd got down to the Pier Head a lot more people were up and about including a policeman who eyed us suspiciously. ''Ello, 'Ello, 'Ello' he said 'and where are you two going so early in the morning?' 'Fishing' I said. 'Train spotting' said Midge and we looked at each other. 'Just as long as you're not running away to sea' said the policeman. 'Oh no' we chorused 'just as if we would.' He winked at us. 'Off you go then and remember to look both ways before crossing your eyes.' We ran off and straight down to the landing stage where a lot of ships were tied up. There was no time to lose because already quite a few were putting out to sea.

Adapted from *The Stowaways* by Roger McGough

Using apostrophes: revision

Remember that apostrophes are used for two reasons:

1 To show where letters have been missed out (omission):

Do not → don't   I have → I've

2 To show someone owns something (possession):

Karen's jacket is torn and the boys' jumpers are ripped.

Did you notice that the apostrophe is in a different place in the words *Karen's* and *boys'*? This is because there is only one Karen but several boys.

To know where to put the apostrophe, ask yourself: How many owners are there?

If there is only one owner, just add an apostrophe and -s:

the CD belonging to Tim → Tim's CD

If there is more than one owner, look carefully at the plural word being used.

- **If the plural ends in -s**, just add an apostrophe:

  the bags belonging to the <u>twins</u> → the twins' bags

- **If the plural does not end in -s**, add an apostrophe and -s:

  the books belonging to the <u>women</u> → the women's books

9.3

Rewrite the sentences below, putting in apostrophes.

1 'Weve got to get one more goal. Im sure we can do it!' said Steve.

2 At last Steves team scored. Theyd won the Cup!

3 All the players faces were dripping with sweat.

4 The captains shirt was ripped.

5 The mens shorts were covered in mud.

6 The crowd cheered and shouted, 'Youve done it! Youre the champions!'

Writing speech

9.4

Read the cartoons. Then look at how the conversation in the first picture is written out, below.

Open speech marks.

Use a capital letter after the speech marks.

Put punctuation before closing the speech marks.

Start each speech on a new line.

> "And what time of night do you call this?" asked Danni, pointing to her watch.
> Mum replied, "Sorry, I tried to call you but the phone box was vandalised."

Put a comma in front of the speech marks when the speech is part of a sentence.

9.5

Follow the rules to write out Danni's speech in the second cartoon.

9.6

Now write *Mum said* and write out Mum's speech in the second cartoon. Follow the rules above.

9.7

Make up the rest of the conversation between Danni and Mum. Follow the rules so that you punctuate it correctly.

"What about your mobile phone?" asked ...

TRF
PAGE 51
SKILLS
PAGE 28

Setting out quotations

9.8

To answer a question you may need to quote from a text.
The box below shows you how to set out quotations.

1 Quotations of one to three words can be written as part of the sentence:

Quotation marks.

The words 'wet fish' make you think of something cold and damp.

2 Quotations of four or more words go on a new line:

Use a comma or colon
before the quotation.

Punctuation marks at
the end of a quotation
go before the closing
quotation mark.

The text shows Mel is very cold:
   'Mel was ... as cold as a wet fish on a slab.'

Start about one
centimetre in.

Open quotation
mark.

Use three dots (an ellipsis) like this if
you are missing out some words.

Always make sure you copy the words from the text exactly. If you are quoting
poetry then set the words out on the page exactly as the poet did.

9.9

TRF
PAGE 52
SKILLS
PAGE 21

**Read the passage below. Then answer the questions.
Make sure you set out the quotations correctly.**

Mel was now cold to the touch – as cold as a wet fish on a slab.
Even in Angel's waterproof jacket Mel did not give out any heat
of his own. Angel knew Mel must not be allowed to fall asleep, he
must be kept awake.

Adapted from *Forever X* by Geraldine McCaughrean

1 Which words show that Mel is cold?

2 Explain how the author shows that Mel is ill. Choose two
quotations from the text to help you.

Spelling: sight rhymes

TRF
PAGE 56
SKILLS
PAGE 11

Some words end in the same group of letters but they may be *said* differently. Words like this are called **sight rhymes**. Read these sentences. Listen to how you say the words in **bold**.

*He didn't **cough although** he was feeling **rough**.*

9.10

Copy down each pair of sentences below. Choose sight rhymes from the box to fill the blanks.

1 *a)* _____ the sea was calm, many boats were at sea.

  b) There was just _____ wind to keep them moving.

2 *a)* Jo _____ by the window in the coastguard station.

  b) Dave seemed in a really bad _____.

3 *a)* She handed Dave a _____ of soapy water.

  b) Dave gave her a _____ and turned away.

4 *a)* Jo did not want to _____ with him so went outside.

  b) A _____ flew over and started to drink the water.

although row bowl enough mood crow scowl stood

9.11

Work in pairs. Each of you chooses a box. Read out the sentences from your box to your partner. Four words are sight rhymes. Your partner must write them down.

1 Throw me the ball!
Don't hit the cow.
I've banged my elbow.
How did you do that?

2 Did you read today's results?
Our school is in the lead.
The Head is really pleased!
Last time it was a dead heat.

Spelling: homophones

TRF
PAGE 57
SKILLS
PAGE 23

Some words are *spelled* differently but still *sound* the same. Words like these are called **homophones**.

Read these sentences. Listen to how you say the words in bold.

Stand here!

Can you hear me?

9.12

Copy the sentences below. Choose the correct word to fill the blanks.

1 Cut the bread on the bread _____ (bored/board).

2 I wish I _____ (knew/new) where the strawberry jam is.

3 Will you buy some more _____ (cereal/serial) for me?

4 It's a very dark _____ (knight/night).

5 I don't think it's _____ (fair/fare) to give Kevin the prize.

9.13

Write sentences showing what each word in the groups below means. Use a dictionary if you need help.

1 here/hear

2 weather/whether

3 their/they're/there

4 too/to/two

5 pair/pear

6 waist/waste

7 know/no

8 passed/past

9 peace/piece

10 through/threw

Spelling: common mistakes

9.14
TRF
PAGES 78–79
SKILLS
PAGES 60–61

The following words are often spelled incorrectly. Write a sentence which includes each word. Underline the parts of the words which are most difficult to remember.

1 separate	2 desperate	3 beautiful
4 necessary	5 friend	6 occasion
7 because	8 business	9 accommodation
10 disappear	11 doesn't	12 argument
13 Wednesday	14 remember	15 speech

9.15

Use rhymes and memory tricks to remember how to spell difficult words. Write your own for the words above.

For example: **friend**: have a fri**end** until the **end**.
business: there's a **bus in busin**ess.

9.16

Some words can be confused with others which have a similar sound or spelling.

1 Make a list of words you have this difficulty with. Start with these words:

where/were know/now it's/its our/are

2 Learn the words. Write a sentence for each word to show that you understand what it means. Use a dictionary if you need to check spelling or meaning.

For example: **Where** are you going? The shops **were** closed.

Heinemann Educational
Halley Court, Jordan Hill, Oxford OX2 8 EJ
Part of Harcourt Education

Heinemann is the registred trademark of
Harcourt Education Limited

First published 1999

2008 2007
13 12 11 10 9 8

10 digit ISBN: 0 435 10543 4
13 digit ISBN: 978 0 435 10543 3

Designed and typeset by Gecko Ltd
Illustrated by Phil Healey, Desmond Nicholas, Andrew Quelch, Gary Wing and Gecko Ltd.
Photo research: Thelma Gilbert
Cover design by MCC
Printed and bound by Scotprint

Acknowledgements
The Publishers and Clare Constant dedicate this Series in warm memory of Sue Duberley, with gratitude for all that she gave of herself in her teaching and writing.

The Authors and Publishers thank Lisa Roberts for her contribution to Units 8 and 9 of this book, and are most grateful to David Robinson for his consultancy on the grammar content in this course. Clare Constant thanks Shirley Wakley for her professionalism, enthusiasm and commitment in the preparation of this course, and all the Heinemann 'team' for their invaluable input.

This book is dedicated with all our love to Madeleine Clare Constant – who ran to her own production schedule.

The Authors and Publishers would like to thank the following for permission to use copyright material.

Penguin Books Australia Ltd for an adapted extract from 'Licked' in *Unbearable* by Paul Jennings, page 7; D.C. Thomson & Co, for the article 'Get Rich Tips' from *Shout* magazine, No. 117, August 1997, page 9; The Big Issue for the poem 'How much?' by Pete from Brighton, July 1998, page 11; Transworld Publishers Ltd for an adapted extract from *Pig-Heart Boy* by Malorie Blackman (Corgi, a division of Transworld Publishers Ltd) copyright © by Oneta Malorie Blackman 1997, all rights reserved, page 15, and for an adapted extract from *girls in love* by Jacqueline Wilson (Doubleday, a division of Transworld Publishers Ltd) copyright © by Jacqueline Wilson 1997, all rights reserved, page 25; Robert Sparrow for the poem 'Having My Ears Done', page 17; SmithKline Beecham plc for the advertisement 'There is only one drink accredited by the British Dental Association', page 19; Solo Syndication Ltd on behalf of the *Daily Mail* for an extract from the article 'Emma's Party' by Chris Brooke, 24 June 1998, page 27; Little, Brown and Company (UK) for the poem 'Break Dance' by Grace Nichols, page 29 from *Lazy Thoughts of a Lazy Woman* (Virago Press), and for an adapted extract from *Three Moons in Vietnam* by Maria Coffey, page 57, Walker Books Ltd for an adapted extract from *The Nature of the Beast* by Janni Howker, page 35, copyright © Janni Howker 1985; BBC Wildlife Magazine for extracts from the article 'Acts of Cruelty' July 1998, by Danny Penman, page 37; David Higham Associates on behalf of Anne Fine for an extract from *The Granny Project*, page 45; The BBC for an extract from the script of the programme 'Here and Now', page 47, broadcast 1 June 1998: Mrs Judith Summerfield for the poem 'Ess'ole' by Geoffrey Summerfield, page 49; Abner Stein on behalf of Ray Bradbury for an adapted extract from *The Pedestrian*, in *The Golden Apples of the Sun*, page 55; Faber and Faber Ltd for the poem 'The Harvest Moon', page 59, from *Season's Songs* by Ted Hughes; Sheil Land Associates Ltd on behalf of Susan Hill for an extract from *I'm the King of the Castle* (Penguin Books) copyright © Susan Hill 1970, page 77; Peters, Fraser & Dunlop Ltd on behalf of Roger McGough for an adapted extract from *The Stowaways*, page 89; Oxford University Press for an extract from *Forever X.* by Geraldine McCaughrean 1997, page 93.

The Publishers have made every effort to trace the copyright holders, but if they have inadvertently overlooked any, they will be pleased to make the necessary arrangements at the first opportunity.

The Publishers would like to thank the following for permission to reproduce photographs on the pages noted.

Stock Directory, p9; Ribena Tooth Kind, p19; Sally & Richard Greenhill, p23; Will Lack, p27; Rex Features, p33; Advertising Archives, p37; Rex Features pp40, 43; Roger Scruton, p47; Hulton Getty, p53; Performing Arts Library/Clive Barda, p75; Fred Olsen, p81.